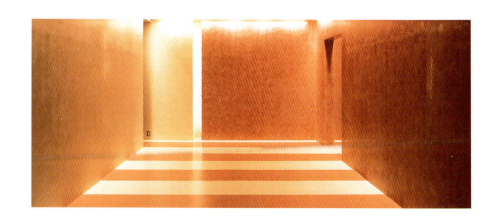

Page 3 · Seite 3
Glasstation Ova, Aoyama, Tokyo, 1991
Photo: Nacása & Partners Inc.

This book was printed on 100% chlorine-free bleached paper in accordance with the TCF standard.

© 1996 Benedikt Taschen Verlag GmbH
Hohenzollernring 53, D-50672 Köln
© 1996 STUDIO 80
1-17-14 Minami-Aoyama, Minato-ku, Tokyo 107 Japan
Tel 81-3-3479-5071 Fax 81-3-3475-4586

Authors: Shigeru Uchida, Ikuyo Mitsuhashi, Toru Nishioka, Studio 80, Aldo Rossi
Design and Layout: Yoshitsuyo Noma
Project Management: Kiyoshi Hasebe, Izumi Suzuki, Minako Morita
English translation: Alfred Birnbaum, Toyota Horiguchi, Morris Adjmi
Minako Morita, World Bridge Corporation
German translation: Alexander Sahm
French translation: Jacques Bosser

Printed in Italy
ISBN 3-8228-8597-5

Interior Design

Uchida, Mitsuhashi,
Nishioka & Studio 80
Vol. II

TASCHEN

KÖLN LISBOA LONDON NEW YORK OSAKA PARIS

Contents | Inhalt | Sommaire

Works | Werke | Œuvres

39   JI-AN, GYO-AN, SO-AN

46   AOYAMA-MIHONCHO

50   ITCHOH

52   KITAJIMA

54   HORIZONTAL

55   VERTICAL Series

56   STORMY WEATHER

57   EAST OF THE SUN

60   MISS ASHIDA

62   MISS ASHIDA

64   GLASSTATION OVA

68   ASABA KATSUMI DESIGN STUDIO

72   COLUMN

73   untitled

74   AUGUST Chair

78   CONVERSATION

80   A TANTOT

81   KIE

82   FURUKAWA RESIDENCE

88   HIGURASHI RESIDENCE

93   COME RAIN, COME SHINE

94   DAY BY DAY

95   RAMONA

98   Xstage IM Series

104 SEPTEMBER

105 DEAR FAUSTO

108 DEAR VERA

109 DEAR MORRIS

112 HOTEL IL PALAZZO

118 ASAHI BEER GUEST ROOM

123 LA RANARITA

130 BUSHOAN

132 ORIJINZA

136 KIMIKO BY KIMIKO

138 untitled

139 untitled

140 MIRAI-CHASHITSU

144 NIJO-DAIME SHIN

146 NIJO-DAIME SO

149 Major Works

Essay | Essay | Essai

8   Homage to Uchida

10   The Bounds of Privacy

42   Toward a New Tea-Room

58   Design and Everyday Life

76   Interior Design Work

96   Xstage IM Series

110 Hotel Il Palazzo

128 Bushoan

142 Shikimi

Homage to Uchida

Aldo Rossi

If we were to discuss the work of Apollinaire, it would be difficult to talk about a particular work; instead, we see it reflected in all of modern French and European art. This came to mind when I was asked to write about Uchida. I thought that my good fortune in having known him as a friend was for me of greater importance than the artistic value of his work.

In his life as in his work, Uchida begins with a clear idea that recalls the secret of the world of Zen. But then he does not remain sealed

Hommage an Uchida

Aldo Rossi

Wollte man das Werk Apollinaires analysieren, würde es schwerfallen, sich auf eine einzige seiner Schriften zu beschränken; schließlich beeinflußte es die gesamte französische und europäische Kunst der Moderne. Dieser Gedanke kam mir, als ich gebeten wurde, über Uchida zu schreiben. Ihn als Freund zu haben, ist für mich von weit größerer Bedeutung als der künstlerische Wert seiner Arbeit. Leben und Werk Uchidas gründen in einer klaren Idee, die an das Geheimnis des Zen erinnert. Doch läßt er sich durch dieses Geheimnis nicht

Hommage à Uchida

Aldo Rossi

Si nous devions discuter de l'importance de l'œuvre d'Apollinaire, il serait difficile de parler d'un texte en particulier, et pourtant, nous voyons qu'elle se reflète dans la totalité de l'art moderne français et européen. Cette idée me vint lorsque l'on me demanda d'écrire sur Uchida. Je pensai alors que le bonheur de l'avoir connu comme ami était pour moi d'une importance encore plus grande que la valeur artistique de son travail. Dans sa vie comme dans son œuvre, Uchida part toujours d'une idée simple et claire qui rappelle l'univers

within this secret but rather loves to follow the path of the work itself; he hears the different sounds, gathers different suggestions, so as to return to himself.

And so it was in my encounter with him that I understood how silly it is to talk about oriental and occidental cultures. Understanding is easy when people remain themselves, but at the same time are not closed in on themselves. In a joint project, Hotel Il Palazzo in Fukuoka, I had the opportunity to work with Uchida and Morris Adjmi. The former is Japanese and the latter is American. In some ways, at least for me, there was an effort to express the beauty of the Orient even if perhaps I was asked for the opposite, that is: to be as Italian as the name of the building – Il Palazzo – demanded. I consider this building to be quite beautiful. It became a grand new architecture through its Italian monumentality, great New York walls, and a secretive Japanese beauty. Uchida always smiles when confronted with difficulties; he smiles knowingly, like the ancient monks who knew how difficult peace is. That is what I want to say about him. I feel it is more important to bear witness than to offer a judgment on what he has done: everyone can see its beauty and an artist's work speaks for itself. I have written all of this out of admiration and friendship, and I do not know how to separate these feelings.

binden, sondern liebt es vielmehr, dem vom Werk eingeschlagenen Weg zu folgen; er hört verschiedenartige Geräusche, bekommt mannigfaltige Anstöße und findet so zu sich selbst zurück.

Meine Begegnung mit Uchida machte mir bewußt, wie töricht die Unterscheidung zwischen östlichen und westlichen Kulturen ist. Gegenseitiges Verständnis fällt dann leicht, wenn die Menschen sich selbst treu bleiben, sich jedoch offen gegenüber anderen zeigen. Bei einem gemeinsamen Projekt, dem Hotel Il Palazzo in Fukuoka, hatte ich Gelegenheit, mit Uchida und Morris Adjmi zusammenzuarbeiten, einem Japaner und einem Amerikaner. Ich bemühte mich dabei, die Schönheit des Orients zum Ausdruck zu bringen, auch wenn vielleicht das genaue Gegenteil von mir erwartet wurde, d.h. so italienisch zu sein, wie der Name des Gebäudes – Il Palazzo – es erforderte. Das Ergebnis repräsentiert für mich eine großartige neue Architektur durch ihre italienische Monumentalität, die grandiosen New Yorker Vertikalen und ihre geheimnisvolle japanische Schönheit. Immer wenn Uchida mit Schwierigkeiten konfrontiert wird, lächelt er; es ist ein wissendes Lächeln und gleicht jenem der Mönche vergangener Zeiten, die wußten, wie schwierig Frieden ist. Das ist es, was ich über Uchida sagen möchte. Ich finde es wichtiger, Zeuge seines Schaffens zu sein, als ein Urteil darüber zu fällen, denn das Werk eines Künstlers spricht für sich. Ich habe all dies aus Bewunderung und Freundschaft geschrieben und weiß auch nicht, wie ich diese Gefühle auseinanderhalten könnte.

secret du Zen. Mais il n'en reste pas pour autant confiné dans ce secret, et préfère laisser l'œuvre elle-même suivre son cours ; il sait entendre des sons différents, rassembler des impressions différentes de façon à toujours se retrouver lui-même.

C'est ainsi que j'ai compris à travers cette rencontre combien il était stupide de toujours parler de cultures orientale et occidentale. Se comprendre est facile lorsque les gens restent eux-mêmes, et qu'en même temps ils ne restent pas renfermés sur eux-mêmes. Lors d'un projet commun, l'hôtel Il Palazzo à Fukuoka, j'ai eu l'opportunité de travailler avec Uchida et Morris Adjmi. Le premier est japonais, le second américain. D'une certaine façon, il y avait le souci de ma part d'exprimer la beauté de l'Orient même si l'on attendait peut-être de moi le contraire, c'est-à-dire d'être aussi italien que le laissait entendre le nom du bâtiment – Il Palazzo. Je pense que ce bâtiment remarquable s'est imposé comme une grande et nouvelle architecture grâce à sa monumentalité italienne, ses grands murs à la new-yorkaise, et sa beauté secrète japonaise. Uchida sourit toujours quand il se trouve confronté à des difficultés ; il sourit pour de bonnes raisons, comme cet ancien moine qui savait à quel point la paix était difficile. C'est ce que j'ai envie de dire à son sujet. Je sens qu'il est plus important de porter témoignage que de proposer un jugement sur ce qu'il a fait. Tout le monde peut admirer la beauté, et l'œuvre d'un artiste parle d'elle-même. J'ai écrit tout cela par admiration et par amitié, et je ne sais comment faire la part entre ces deux sentiments.

The Bounds of Privacy: Boundary and Domain in Japanese Culture
Shigeru Uchida

Edited from a lecture delivered at the
11 November 1994 symposium
3rd Yokohama Big Design

My topic today is potentially a problematic and also very interesting subject. No doubt the word "privacy" conjures up an image of a "self" surrounded by an invisible barrier that cuts it off from all others, but such a scheme of "self" just does not seem to be found in Japan.

Rather, I would like to discuss the notion of "boundaries" in terms of the more succinct expression, *kekkai*. Originally a Buddhist concept, a *kekkai* was said to exist at the divide between the sacred and the profane, in which the profane was in essence

Die Grenzen des Privaten: Raum und Begrenzung in der japanischen Kultur
Shigeru Uchida

Niederschrift eines Vortrags beim Symposion
3rd Yokohama Big Design
am 11. November 1994

In meinem Vortrag geht es um ein problematisches, aber sehr interessantes Thema. Zweifellos wird mit dem Wort »Privatsphäre« das Bild eines »Ich« heraufbeschworen, das durch eine unsichtbare Barriere von allen anderen Menschen abgetrennt ist. In Japan scheint es eine solche Vorstellung vom »Ich« nicht zu geben. Daher möchte ich den Begriff der »Grenze« anhand der präziseren japanischen Bezeichnung *kekkai* untersuchen. Der ursprünglich buddhistische Begriff besagte, ein *kekkai* existiere an der Scheide zwischen dem Heiligen

Les limites de l'intimité : Le champ et la limite dans la culture japonaise
Shigeru Uchida

D'après une conférence donnée lors du
symposium du 11 novembre 1994
3rd Yokohama Big Design

Mon sujet d'aujourd'hui recouvre une problématique d'une grande richesse potentielle. Il est évident que le mot « intimité » évoque l'image d'un « moi » enfermé derrière une barrière invisible qui le sépare des autres, mais qu'un tel type de « moi » semble difficile à identifier dans la société japonaise.

Je préfèrerais plutôt parler de « limite », dans le sens de ce que recouvre l'expression plus succincte de *kekkai*. Concept bouddhiste à l'origine, on disait qu'un *kekkai* existait à la frontière séparant le sacré du profane. Le

10

an analogue – a continuum – through which crop up sacred times, places and persons. Such sacred "moments" are digital – that is, discrete isolates. It is within this structure, where cutting out demarcations in linear time-space allows transcendent elements to emerge, that I see the very source of the "self".

Ego, subject, "self". But what is this "self" that perceives a "world" here and now, that dwells within that "world"? Irrational as it seems, it is conceivable only as an in-bounded "non-world" set off from the "world".

Granted, the idea of carving a small, exclusive sub-area out of that continuous world-space bears an undeniably close relation to the idea of "self". And of course, the act of fencing something off relates closely to that of possessing. Yet surely the concepts of "sacred" and "profane", not to mention the very means of demarcating their boundaries, must vary greatly with their respective cultural contexts. No doubt such distinctions had their beginnings in erecting physical barriers between either side, so that what lay within these barriers or without

und dem Profanen, wobei das Profane ein sozusagen Analoges sei – ein Kontinuum –, durch das heilige Zeit-räume, Orte und Personen hervor-scheinen. Solche heiligen »Momente« hingegen seien digital, d.h. vereinzelt und isoliert. Innerhalb dieser Struktur, in der das Herauslösen von Abschnitten aus dem linearen Raum-Zeit-Gefüge das Hervortreten trans-zendenter Elemente ermöglicht, sehe ich den Ursprung des »Ich«.

Ego, Subjekt, »Ich«. Doch was ist die-ses »Ich«, das eine »Welt« im Hier und Jetzt wahrnimmt und sich in dieser

»Welt« einrichtet? So irrational es auch scheinen mag, das »Ich« ist nur faßbar als eine außerweltlich von Welt eingeschlossene »Nicht-Welt«. Unbe-streitbar besteht eine enge Beziehung zwischen der Vorstellung eines aus dem kontinuierlichen Welt-Raum her-ausgeschnittenen, kleinen und exklu-siven Bereichs und der des »Ich«. Und natürlich sind das Abgrenzen und das Besitzen gleichfalls nahe Verwandte. Allerdings ist, was unter »heilig« und »profan« begriffen wird, und sind erst recht die bloßen Mittel zur Festlegung ihrer Grenzen stark abhängig vom

kekkai était par essence analogue – un *continuum* –, à travers lequel surgis-saient des instants, des lieux et des personnes sacrés. De tels « moments » sacrés sont digitaux, c'est-à-dire des éléments isolés. C'est dans cette structure, où des interruptions dans les démarcations du temps-espace linéaire permettent à des éléments transcendants d'émerger, que je vois la source même du « moi ».

Ego, sujet, « moi ». Mais qu'est-ce que ce « moi » qui perçoit un « monde » ici et là, et qui loge à l'intérieur de ce « monde » ?

Aussi irrationnel que cela puisse paraître, il n'est concevable que comme un « non-monde » enfermé, séparé du « monde ». Accordons que l'idée de se creuser une petite niche bien à soi dans un monde-espace continu offre une indéniable ressemblance avec l'idée de « moi ». Et bien sûr, l'acte d'isoler quelque chose par des barrières ressemble de très près à la possession. Et tout aussi sûrement, les concepts de « sacré » et de « profane », sans même rappeler les moyens mêmes de démarquer leurs frontières, doivent grandement varier

stood as utterly disparate dimensions. Eventually, such spatial registers became less physical and more emblematic devices, that is, mere perceptual constructs. Fixed rigid barriers are not absolutely necessary where some form of notational index will suffice. I will touch upon this point again later.

Spatial Awareness via Verbalised Domains

As I see it, notions of privacy and its bounds are deeply rooted in the cosmologies of particular cultures. Hence any Japanese scheme of demarcating boundaries based on Japan's native cosmological premises will differ vastly from that of Western societies. This is an important consideration to bear in mind.

In order to reflect upon typically Japanese spaces, I would like to examine "*kekkai* constructs" or "bounded domains". I should emphasize that I am not speaking of *kekkai* strictly in the Buddhist sense, but rather more generally as a small, circumscribed space.

As is frequently pointed out, human

---

kulturellen Kontext. Diese Unterscheidung konnte erst in dem Augenblick getroffen werden, als mit der Errichtung physischer Barrieren zwischen den Seiten all das, was sich jenseits der Grenzen befand, plötzlich für etwas vollkommen Fremdes einstehen mußte. Schließlich verloren die räumlichen Einheiten ihre physische Qualität und wurden zu eher sinnbildlichen Hilfsmitteln, d. h. wahrnehmungsbestimmten Konstrukten. Starre und strikte Barrieren sind nicht unbedingt notwendig, wenn die gleiche Funktion auch von einer Art gespeicherten Zeichensystem übernommen werden kann. Ich werde auf diesen Punkt später noch zurückkommen.

Raumwahrnehmung durch benannte Bereiche

Nach meiner Auffassung sind die Vorstellungen von Privatsphäre und ihren Grenzen tief im Weltbild der jeweiligen Kulturen verwurzelt. Demnach müssen sich alle auf das spezifische Weltbild Japans gründenden Modelle der Grenzfestlegung erheblich von solchen westlicher Gesellschaften

---

dans le cadre de leurs contextes culturels respectifs. Il est certain que de telles distinctions trouvent leur origine dans l'élévation, de chaque côté, de barrières physiques afin que ce qui se trouve de part et d'autre de cette barrière soit perçu comme appartenant à des dimensions différentes. Par la suite, de tels registres spatiaux devinrent de moins en moins physiques mais emblématiques, ou, en d'autres termes, des constructions de la perception. Il n'est pas absolument nécessaire d'élever des barrières rigides lorsqu'une certaine forme d'indication peut suffire. Je reviendrai sur ce point.

La conscience de l'espace à travers la verbalisation

A mon sens, les notions de l'intimité et de ses limites sont profondément enracinées dans la cosmologie de chaque culture prise séparément. C'est ainsi que les schémas japonais de démarcation de frontières basées sur les prémisses cosmologiques indigènes du Japon différeront grandement de ceux des sociétés occidentales. Cette importante

beings do not perceive the world as it is. The act of naming always enters into the picture, as do what I have termed *kekkai* constructs. We can only grasp the entirety of the world when it is divided up into more concrete spaces by various *kekkai* or demarcations.

That is to say, our living environment is full of boundaries, as well as the domains that these various boundaries establish. Furthermore, our spatial awareness depends upon verbalisation of such demarcated domains. Differences between the various human means of carving out spaces or their verbalisation are among the best indicators of cultural differences between peoples. At the very least, *kekkai* constructs or bounded domains are in no way universals common to all ethnicities the world over.

Let us consider myths of "inside" versus "outside". The act of making a boundary necessarily frames a duality composed of a closed "inner" realm and an excluded "outer" realm. Herein we see a *kekkai* or boundary formed at the dichotomy or contrast between the order (cosmos) within the com-

unterscheiden. Diese Überlegung verdient besondere Beachtung.

In Hinblick auf eine Untersuchung typisch japanischer Räume, möchte ich mich zunächst »*kekkai*-Konstrukten« oder »abgegrenzten Bereichen« zuwenden. Ich sollte vorausschicken, daß von *kekkai* nicht im streng buddhistischen Sinn die Rede sein wird, sondern in dem allgemeineren eines kleinen umschriebenen Raumes.

Es wird häufig darauf hingewiesen, daß die Menschen die Welt nicht unmittelbar wahrnehmen. Der Akt des Benennens führt stets zu einem Bild, wie es auch das tut, was ich als *kekkai*-Konstrukte bezeichne. Wir können die Gesamtheit der Welt nur dann erfassen, wenn sie durch mannigfaltige *kekkai* oder Grenzlinien in konkretere Räume unterteilt ist.

Daraus folgt, daß sich unsere Lebenswelt aus zahllosen Grenzen zusammensetzt sowie aus den Bereichen, die jene Grenzen konstituieren. Darüber hinaus ist unsere Raumwahrnehmung auf die Benennung solcherart abgegrenzter Bereiche angewiesen. Die unterschiedlichen Methoden der Menschen, Räume oder deren Verba-

considération ne doit surtout pas être négligée.

Dans ma réflexion sur les espaces typiquement japonais, je voudrais examiner les « constructions *kekkai* » ou « champs limités ». Je dois faire remarquer que je ne parle pas du *kekkai* au sens strictement bouddhiste, mais plus généralement d'un petit espace circonscrit.

Comme on le note fréquemment, les êtres humains ne perçoivent pas le monde en tant que tel. Toujours intervient l'acte de nommer, c'est ainsi que je parle de constructions *kekkai* ou de champs limités. Nous ne pouvons appréhender la globalité du monde que lorsque celle-ci est divisée en espaces plus concrets au moyen de différents *kekkai* ou par des lignes de démarcations.

C'est dire que l'environnement de notre vie est rempli de multiples limites et des multiples champs que ces différentes frontières établissent. De plus, notre conscience spatiale dépend de la verbalisation des domaines ainsi démarqués. Les différences entre les divers moyens humains de déterminer des espaces

Garden of Jisho-ji Temple (Ginkakuji Temple), Kyoto
Garten des Jisho-ji-Tempels (Ginkakuji-Tempel), Kyoto
Jardin du temple Jisho-ji (temple Ginkakuji), Kyoto

munity and the confusion (chaos) without. In most cases, the origins of boundary myths are to be found in a fear of the unknown, the foreignness of what lies outside the sedentary farming community. Such mythologized fears of the dark world outside serve to set up *kekkai*, which in turn cement the "sameness" of whatever lies inside while underscoring the "otherness" of all else outside. Relationships between those within the community and those without, between the interior and exterior of the house, between one room and another, would all seem to manifest the distinct cultural values of a given people. Just as it is certainly true that our post-19th-century way of life has come about through the dissolution of such myths. Yet if we look carefully, we can often detect such cultural roots surfacing even in contemporary society.

Thus we can see why *kekkai* constructs are so closely linked to the cosmology of each culture. As long as human beings put names to things so as to make the world their own, cultures with different languages, cultures with

lisierung herauszulösen, gehören zu den besten Indikatoren kultureller Differenzen.

Wenden wir uns den Mythen von »Innen« und »Außen« zu. Der Akt einer Grenzziehung stellt notwendigerweise eine Dualität her, die aus einem umschlossenen »inneren« und einem ausgeschlossenen »äußeren« Bezirk besteht. Hier erkennen wir ein *kekkai*, eine Grenze, die sich an der Dichotomie oder dem Kontrast zwischen der Ordnung (Kosmos) innerhalb der Gemeinschaft und der Konfusion (Chaos) außerhalb herausgebildet hat. Fast immer lassen sich die Ursprünge der Grenzmythen auf die Angst vor dem Unbekannten zurückführen, der Fremdheit dessen, was außerhalb der seßhaft gewordenen, bäuerlichen Gemeinschaft liegt. Solche mythologischen Ängste vor der äußeren dunklen Welt dienen der Errichtung von *kekkai*, welche wiederum die »Gleichheit« von allem Innengelegenen und die »Andersheit« von allem Außengelegenen festschreiben.

Die Beziehungen zwischen den Mitgliedern einer Gemeinschaft und den

et leur verbalisation sont parmi les meilleurs indicateurs des différences culturelles entre les peuples. Le moins que l'on puisse dire, c'est que les constructions *kekkai* ou champs limités ne sont en aucun cas communs aux multiples groupes ethniques qui peuplent l'univers.

Considérons les mythes de « l'intérieur » contre « l'extérieur ». L'acte de tracer une limite encadre nécessairement une dualité composée d'un champ « intérieur » et d'un champ « extérieur », qui est exclu. Ainsi voyons-nous un *kekkai*, ou une frontière, se former par contraste entre l'ordre (cosmos) à l'intérieur de la communauté, et la confusion (chaos) hors d'elle. Dans la plupart des cas, les origines des mythes liés aux limites résident dans la crainte de l'inconnu, de l'étrangeté, de ce qui s'étend hors la communauté fermière sédentaire. De telles peurs mythologiques du monde obscur extérieur servent à élever un *kekkai*, qui, en retour, cimente « l'identité » de tout ce qui se trouve à l'intérieur tout en mettant en évidence « l'altérité » de tout ce qui est extérieur.

divergent spatial percepts will necessarily differ in their versions of the world. Let us now turn to the subject of cosmology and privacy, mainly in Japanese architectural space, in terms of various schemes of spatial partitioning.

Physical *kekkai* and *kekkai* Devices
I find three different classes of *kekkai* constructs here in Japan. The first is that of "physical *kekkai*". These are fixed and not easily moved – *kekkai* as obstacles. They are what we might also call "brute *kekkai*". The inside of

the barrier is quite visibly cut off from the outside and any communication in-between is obstructed. The Great Wall of China is a prime example, but we might also cite the walled cities of Asia Minor, such as Troy, as well as Dubrovnik in former Yugoslavia. Fortress walls were put up to protect the inhabitants from barbarian invasion. Physical structures completely surrounded the space. This is the most basic pattern of *kekkai* construct, the starting point from which humanity – we Japanese included – began to enclose space.

Außenstehenden, zwischen dem Inneren und dem Äußeren eines Hauses, zwischen einem Raum und einem anderen scheinen die verschiedenen kulturellen Werte eines Volkes zu manifestieren. Gleichermaßen trifft zu, daß sich unsere moderne Lebensweise nur durch die Auflösung solcher Mythen herausbilden konnte. Bei einer genaueren Betrachtung können wir allerdings Überreste dieser kulturellen Wurzeln oft noch in unserer heutigen Gesellschaft entdecken. Darin zeigt sich, warum *kekkai*-Konstrukte so eng mit dem Weltbild einer

jeden Kultur verbunden sind. Solange Menschen Dinge benennen, um sich die Welt anzueignen, werden Kulturen mit unterschiedlichen Sprachen und voneinander abweichenden Raumvorstellungen diese Welt zwangsläufig verschieden auffassen. Wenden wir uns nun der Untersuchung der Begriffe Weltbild und Privatsphäre zu. Hierbei konzentrieren wir uns vor allem auf die japanische Architektur und deren verschiedenen Modellen von Raum und Raumaufteilung.

Les relations entre ceux qui se trouvent à l'intérieur de la communauté et ceux à l'extérieur, entre l'intérieur et l'extérieur de la maison, entre une pièce et une autre, devraient toutes manifester les valeurs culturelles distinctes d'un peuple donné. De même est-il certain que le style de vie japonais de la période qui succède au XIXᵉ siècle a pu naître à partir de la disparition de mythes de ce genre. Et pourtant, en regardant avec attention, nous pouvons encore déceler de telles racines culturelles, même dans notre société contemporaine.

Ceci nous fait voir pourquoi les constructions *kekkai* sont si étroitement liées à la cosmologie de chaque culture. Aussi longtemps que les êtres humains donneront des noms aux choses afin de mieux contrôler le monde, les cultures de langues différentes, les cultures de perceptions spatiales divergentes différeront nécessairement dans leur vision du monde. Regardons maintenant la cosmologie et l'intimité, principalement dans l'espace architectural japonais, et à travers les différentes solutions apportées à la partition de l'espace.

The second class is that of "*kekkai* devices". From this point we begin to see Japanese cultural tendencies emerging. They may include temporary or moveable elements; or, if architectural in nature, they put up little resistance to physical force. *Ikegaki* (hedges), *magaki* (plaited-bamboo garden fencing), *mon* (gates), *shikimi* (crossbars), *koshi* (lattices), *shoji* (translucent paper sliding doors), *fusuma* (opaque paper sliding doors), *noren* (partition curtains), *shikii* (doorsills), *kutsunugi ishi* ("footware removal" entryway stepstones), and *chozubachi* (stone washbasins) are all typical examples of such devices. Likewise, most means of demarcating temporary ceremonial or festival grounds may by extension be considered *kekkai* devices. The Shinto *shimenawa* (sacred straw rope), which derives its name from *shimesu* "to show" – or possibly from *shimeru* "to occupy" or the homophonic *shimeru* "to tie" – thus carries the meaning of a "sign", a "hold", or a "close".

Sacred or holy precincts are often roped off with *shimenawa*. One can often see four bamboo posts set up by

Materielle *kekkai* und instrumentelle *kekkai*

Meines Erachtens kann man in Japan drei Kategorien von *kekkai*-Konstrukten unterscheiden. Die erste Kategorie möchte ich als »materielle *kekkai*« definieren; diese sind starr und relativ unbeweglich – *kekkai* als Hindernisse. Wir können sie auch »harte *kekkai*« nennen. Das Innen ist mittels einer Barriere sichtbar vom Außen abgetrennt, jegliche Kommunikation zwischen den Bereichen ist ausgeschlossen. Hervorragende Beispiele hierfür sind die Chinesische Mauer und ummauerte Städte in Kleinasien wie Troja oder Dubrovnik im ehemaligen Jugoslawien. Wallanlagen wurden errichtet, um die Bevölkerung vor dem Einfall von Barbaren zu schützen. Physisch manifeste Konstruktionen umgaben das gesamte Territorium. Es handelt sich hierbei um das fundamentalste *kekkai*-Konstrukt, den Ausgangspunkt, von dem aus die Menschheit, darunter wir Japaner, begann, Räume zu umschließen.

Die zweite, schon eher spezifisch japanische Kategorie wäre als »instrumentelle *kekkai*« zu bezeichnen. Hierzu

Kekkai physique et techniques *kekkai*

A mon sens, il existe trois différentes catégories de constructions *kekkai* au Japon. La première est le « *kekkai* physique ». Il est fixe, ne se déplace pas facilement, c'est un obstacle. Nous pourrions aussi bien le qualifier de « *kekkai* brut ». Ce qui est à l'intérieur de la barrière est assez visiblement séparé de ce qui se trouve à l'extérieur, et toute communication est impossible. La Grande Muraille de Chine en est un bon exemple, mais l'on pourrait aussi citer les remparts des villes d'Asie Mineure, comme Troie, ou ceux de Dubrovnik en Croatie. Les murs des forteresses furent élevés pour protéger les habitants des invasions barbares, et ces constructions enfermaient complètement l'espace. C'est le type de construction *kekkai* le plus simple, le point de départ à partir duquel l'humanité a commencé à refermer l'espace.

La seconde catégorie est celle des « dispositifs *kekkai* ». C'est ici que nous voyons l'émergence des tendances culturelles japonaises. Elles peuvent inclure des éléments temporaires ou

Ikegaki (hedge) of Jisho-ji Temple (Ginkakuji Temple), Kyoto
Ikégaki (Hecke) des Jisho-ji-Tempels (Ginkakuji-Tempel), Kyoto
Ikégaki (petite haie) du temple Jisho-ji (temple Ginkakuji), Kyoto

Chu-mon (inner gate) and Kuromoji Hedge of Katsura Imperial Palace, Kyoto

Chu-mon (inneres Portal) und Kuromoji-Hecke des Kaiserlichen Katsura-Palastes, Kyoto

Chu-mon (porte intérieure) et haie Kuromoji du palais impérial Katsura, Kyoto

the roadside and strung with *shime-nawa* to create an impromptu sanctuary, frequently for consecrating a building site. Even the act of joining hands at a celebration, or a sumo wrestler who ritually girds (*shimeru*) himself with a loincloth, shows the same degree of signification.

This second class of *kekkai* device is much more subtle than physical *kekkai*. While equally visible, it simultaneously incorporates unseen or tacit demarcations. Let there be no mistake: though the examples I've cited are fairly unambiguous, not everything in this category is so straightforward. Frequently, we find a complex complementarity of interrelationships. Take, for instance, a lattice-work *koshi*, one of the more subtle spatial partitions. Physically, the lattice grid hints at the functions of a wall, yet visually it obstructs nothing at all. It is, in other words, a partitioning device that works on the level of conscious recognition. Here then, is a partitioning device that truly reflects the special character of Japanese spatial concepts. For in Japan, when separating space A from

gehören alle beweglichen oder nur zeitweilig errichteten Elemente sowie solche, die, als Architektur in der Natur, physischer Krafteinwirkung nur wenig Widerstand entgegensetzen. *Ikégaki* (Hecken), *magaki* (geflochtene Bambuszäune), *mon* (Tore), *shikimi* (Querbalken), *koshi* (Lattengitter), *shoji* (durchsichtige Papierschiebetüren), *fusuma* (undurchsichtige Papierschiebetüren), *noren* (Vorhänge zur Raumteilung), *shikii* (Türschwellen), *kutsunugi ishi* (Trittsteine in der Eingangshalle zum Ausziehen der Schuhe) und schließlich *chozubachi* (steinerne Waschbecken) sind typische Beispiele eines solchen Instrumentariums. Ebenso können die meisten Abgrenzungsarten zeitweiliger Kult- oder Feststätten als »instrumentelle *kekkai*« angesehen werden. Das shintoistische *shiménawa*, ein heiliges Seil aus Stroh, das seinen Namen von *shimésu*, »zeigen«, ableitet – vielleicht auch von *shiméru*, »besetzen«, oder von dem homophonen *shiméru*, »binden« –, hat die Bedeutung eines »Zeichens«, das »halt« oder »nicht weiter« signalisieren soll. Heilige Bezirke werden häufig durch *shiménawa* abgeteilt. So

mobiles, ou, s'ils sont de nature architecturale, qui ne présentent que peu de résistance à la force physique. *Ikégaki* (haies), *magaki* (palissades de bambous tressés), *mon* (portes d'entrée), *shikimi* (barres de traverse), *koshi* (treillis), *shoji* (portes coulissantes en papier translucide), *fusuma* (portes coulissantes en papier opaque), *noren* (rideaux de séparation), *shikii* (seuils de portes), *kutsunugi ishi* (marches d'entrée sur lesquelles on se déchausse) et *chozubachi* (bassins de lavage en pierre) sont des exemples typiques de ces dispositifs. De même, la plupart des moyens utilisés pour marquer temporairement les espaces ou les sols de cérémonie et de fête peuvent, par extension, être qualifiés de dispositifs *kekkai*. La *shiménawa* shintoïste (corde de paille sacrée) dont le nom vient de *shimésu*, « montrer », ou peut-être de *shiméru*, « occuper », ou encore de l'homophone *shiméru*, « lier », véhicule ainsi les sens de « signe », de « tenue », ou de « fermeture ». Les espaces sacrés ou saints sont souvent entourés d'une *shiménawa*. On voit souvent au bord d'une route quatre piquets de bam-

space B, instead of fixing a rigid barrier wall, it is also important for each side to know what is going on on the other. This is a connective analogue boundary that both segments and mediates between either side to allow some flow between the two. The *fusuma* door may be closed, but it still provides a hint of what might be going on in the next room. Even the decoration on *fusuma* panels often features some motif that it has in common with the decoration in the adjacent room. This design move clearly reflects an awareness that

spaces A and B are always mutually engaged and interacting.

The cultural bases behind these subtle boundaries, as we will see later when we discuss "suppositional *kekkai*" and "taboo *kekkai*", are replete with complex complementarities.

Domains as Rites of Passage – Marginal Zones

The third category of *kekkai* – which would hardly seem to constitute boundaries at all – are those special Japanese spaces which I will call "marginal zones". These are spaces

kann man beispielsweise an Straßenrändern oft vier Bambuspfosten entdecken, um die *shiménawa* gespannt sind, wodurch ein improvisiertes Heiligtum geschaffen wird, das häufig der Weihe eines potentiellen Baugrundes dient. Auch dem gegenseitigen Händereichen bei einer Zeremonie oder dem sich rituell in ein Lendentuch gürtenden (*shiméru*) Sumo-Ringer kommt ein solcher Bedeutungsgehalt zu.

Das Instrumentarium dieser Kategorie arbeitet viel subtiler als die »materiellen *kekkai*«. Obwohl ebenfalls sichtbar,

umfaßt es auch unsichtbare oder nur im Stillschweigen bestehende Grenzlinien. Um jedem Mißverständnis vorzubeugen: Auch wenn die aufgezählten Beispiele eindeutig sein mögen, so ist doch nicht alles in dieser Kategorie so klar zuzuordnen. Nicht selten stoßen wir auf eine komplexe Folge von einander ergänzenden Beziehungen. Das *koshi* genannte Lattengitter zählt beispielsweise zu den subtileren Arten der Raumaufteilung. Rein materiell deutet es die Funktion einer Wand an, die Sicht versperrt es jedoch nicht. Es handelt sich also um einen

Koshi (lattice) and Shitomi (shade) Separating the Inside and Outside Compounds of Rokuharamitsuji Temple, Kyoto

Koshi (Lattengitter) und Shitomi (Sonnenschutz) zur Unterteilung zwischen dem inneren und dem äußeren Bereich des Rokuharamitsuji-Tempels, Kyoto

Koshi (treillis) et Shitomi (écran) séparant les parties intérieures et extérieures du temple Rokuharamitsuji, Kyoto

bou liés par une *shiménawa* pour créer un sanctuaire temporaire, fréquemment pour consacrer un site de construction. Même l'acte de joindre les mains lors d'une célébration, ou celui du lutteur sumo qui, rituellement, s'entoure (*shiméru*) d'un linge, présente le même degré de signification. Cette seconde catégorie est beaucoup plus subtile que la précédente. Bien que tout aussi visibles, ces dispositifs incorporent simultanément des démarcations tacites ou invisibles. Que l'on ne se trompe pas, même si les exemples que j'ai cités sont assez

clairs, tout ce qui appartient à cette catégorie n'est pas aussi évident. Très souvent, on trouve une complémentarité complexe de relations. Prenons, par exemple, un treillage *koshi*, l'une des partitions les plus subtiles. Physiquement, la grille du treillis remplit les fonctions d'un mur, et pourtant, visuellement, elle n'est pas obstructrice. En d'autres termes, il s'agit d'un dispositif de partition qui agit au niveau d'une reconnaissance consciente. Ici, se trouve donc un dispositif qui reflète parfaitement le caractère spécial des concepts japo-

that arise as passageways from A to B, which relate very closely to both A and B, yet really belong to neither. They are non-A, non-B spaces such as the under-eaves or the *engawa* exposed corridor areas that wrap around traditonal Japanese houses.

By a passageway from A to B, I do not mean merely a momentary transition, but a whole intermediate realm that exists as a rite of passage partaking at once of time and space, that is, a site of initiation. We have seen how myths of inner versus outer, myths of order versus chaos, have their origins in the dichotomies that arise when a community posits a foreign world "out there". A boundary of distinction must be drawn for such myths to arise. *Yashiro* (shrines) and smaller *hokora* (spirit houses), things that are imbued with magic significance and that serve as village boundary markers and furthermore keep out evil spirits, are all *kekkai*. They quite clearly indicate a line, an in-bounding articulation of closure and it is for this reason that we tend to picture *kekkai* divisions as linear demarcations.

Nonetheless, a marginal zone is a

Raumteiler, der auf bewußter Anerkennung beruht. Das *koshi* verdeutlicht somit den speziellen Charakter japanischer Raumauffassung, denn in Japan ist es bei der Abtrennung eines Raumes A von einem Raum B wichtig zu wissen, was sich auf der jeweils anderen beiden Seite zuträgt. Anstelle einer strikten Barriere ist es eine verbindende, analoge Grenze, die die Seiten sowohl segmentiert als auch vermittelt und so einen gewissen Austausch ermöglicht. Die Tür *fusuma* mag geschlossen sein, eine Ahnung von den Vorgängen im Nachbarraum läßt sie dennoch zu. Sogar die Ornamente in den Türfeldern weisen häufig Übereinstimmungen mit den Motiven im angrenzenden Raum auf. In diesem gestalterischen Kunstgriff ist die Überzeugung ausgedrückt, daß sich die Räume A und B immer aufeinander beziehen und interagieren. Die kulturellen Grundlagen solcher subtilen Grenzen sind, wie die Untersuchung der »angenommenen *kekkai*« und der »tabuisierten *kekkai*« noch verdeutlichen wird, von komplex einander ergänzender Faktoren gekennzeichnet.

nais de l'espace, car, au Japon, lorsque l'on sépare un espace A d'un espace B, au lieu d'élever un mur rigide, on considère qu'il est tout aussi important pour chaque côté de savoir ce qui se passe de l'autre. Il s'agit d'une frontière analogique qui réunit deux segments et permet un certain flux d'échange entre eux. La porte *fusuma* peut être fermée, mais elle continue à offrir une sorte d'aperçu sur ce qui peut se passer dans l'autre pièce. Même le décor des panneaux *fusuma* utilise souvent un motif semblable à la décoration de la pièce adjacente.

Cette démarche de design montre clairement la conscience que les espaces A et B sont toujours en interaction l'un avec l'autre. Les bases culturelles sur lesquelles reposent ces subtiles frontières sont riches en complémentarités complexes, comme nous le verrons plus loin lorsque nous parlerons de « *kekkai* supposé » et de « *kekkai* tabou ».

Champs et rites de passage – les zones marginales
La troisième catégorie de *kekkai* – qui, ailleurs, ne constituerait pas le

non-A, non-B space that belongs neither to A nor B. It is, in other words, an unaffiliated "detached" space. And the significance of that "detached" space lies in the rite of passage that sets a non-worldly *hare* (pure) realm apart from the everyday *ke* (defiled) realm. In *chanoyu* – the tea ceremony – to cite one example, we find a ritualistic space that guides us to the tea-room. The *roji* (tea-garden) is just such a space; it is always found paired together with the tea-room. Tea-master Sen Rikyu taught that "it is essential to know *suki* (humility) in the *roji*",

for the activities inside the tea-room constitute an "other world" apart from daily life. To be conducted into that "other world" means casting off worldly affairs and attaining the sphere of *mu* (nothingness) and *ku* (emptiness). And that entails passing through a "detached" marginal zone. It is no coincidence that the ideal to which the rustic tea aesthetic aspired was a "mountain hermitage in the city's midst". That is, an otherworldly refuge imagined far off in the immortal hills yet right in the centre of town.

Bereiche als Riten des Übergangs – Randzonen

Eine dritte Kategorie von *kekkai*, die überhaupt keine Grenzen mehr zu definieren scheint, bilden jene spezifisch japanischen Räume, welche ich als »Randzonen« bezeichnen möchte. Dabei handelt es sich um Räume, die eine »Passage« von A nach B bilden und in enger Beziehung sowohl zu A als auch zu B stehen, letztlich aber zu keinem von beiden gehören. Zu diesen Nicht-A- und Nicht-B-Räumen zählen der Bereich unter einem Dachvorsprung sowie der *engawa*, ein ungeschützter Gang, der das traditionelle japanische Haus umgibt.

Unter »Passage« verstehe ich nicht einen bloß momentanen Übergang, sondern einen ganzen Übergangsbereich, der eine sowohl zeitliche als auch räumliche Existenz besitzt in einem Ritus des »Passierens«, in einer Initiation. Wir haben bereits gesehen, wie die mythischen Gegensatzpaare Innen/Außen und Ordnung/Chaos ihren Ursprung in den Dichotomien haben, die entstehen, wenn eine Gesellschaft eine Welt »außerhalb« postuliert. Solche Mythen sind auf

moindre barrage – relève de ces espaces japonais spéciaux que j'appelle « zones marginales ». Il s'agit d'espaces qui s'étendent de A à B, reliés très étroitement à la fois à A et à B, et qui cependant n'appartiennent ni à l'un ni à l'autre. Ce sont des espaces non-A, non-B, comme, par exemple, la partie sous l'avancée du toit, ou ces couloirs visibles et ouverts – *engawa* – qui entourent les maisons traditionnelles japonaises.

Par un passage de A à B, je ne veux pas parler de simple transition momentanée, mais d'un authentique territoire intermédiaire qui existe en tant que rite de passage relevant du temps et de l'espace, c'est-à-dire un site d'initiation. Nous avons vu comment les mythes de l'intérieur *versus* l'extérieur, de l'ordre *versus* le chaos, trouvent leur origine dans les dichotomies qui se créent lorsqu'une communauté décide qu'un monde étranger est « extérieur ». Une frontière distinctive doit être tracée pour permettre à de tels mythes de prendre naissance. *Yashiro* (sanctuaires) et *hokora* (maisons des esprits, plus petites), objets teintés de signification

Hiroen (open corridor) and South Garden of the Study in the Annex of the Jikoin Temple, Kyoto

Hiroen (offener Gang) und südlicher Garten des Studierzimmers im Anbau des Jikoin-Tempels, Kyoto

Hiroen (couloir ouvert) et jardin Sud pour l'étude dans l'annexe du temple Jikoin, Kyoto

Kutsunugi-Ishi (kutsunugi-stone) at Mikoshiyose of Katsura Imperial Palace, Kyoto

Kutsunugi-Ishi (Kutsunugi-Stein) in Mikoshiyose, Kaiserlicher Katsura-Palast, Kyoto

Kutsunugi-Ishi (pierre kutsunugi) à Mikoshiyose, palais impérial Katsura, Kyoto

Or again, this marginal zone is given architecturally embellished expression in traditional Japanese houses at the under-eaves where the interior extends into the exterior. There most commonly we find the *engawa* and a place for the somewhat ritualized removal of shoes prior to entering the house as is the Japanese custom. In ancient Japan, however, this under-eaves space was more open and natural, while the removal of one's shoes was quite literally a ritual to exorcise the evil forces outside. This space is still strongly external in character, though strictly speaking it is "detached", belonging neither to the exterior nor interior.

This sense of marginal space has contributed greatly to Japanese culture and art. The interior that pushes out toward nature allows a deeper communion with the environment, a more lingering appreciation of beauty. Witness the *Manyoshu* and other ancient Japanese poetic classics abounding with expressions of the spiritual grace of living together with nature.

So much, very simply, for bounding constructs that divide spaces A and B;

unterscheidende Grenzen angewiesen. Die mit magischer Bedeutung aufgeladenen *yashiro* (Schreine) und die kleineren *hokora* (Geisterhäuser) dienen der Markierung von Dorfgrenzen und halten überdies böse Geister fern; beide sind *kekkai*. Wir neigen daher dazu, uns die Unterteilungen durch *kekkai* als Demarkationslinien nur zu verbildlichen.

Nichtsdestotrotz sind es eigenständige, »losgelöste« Räume. Seine Bedeutung erlangt ein »losgelöster« Raum durch den Ritus der »Passage«, der einen überweltlichen, reinen Sektor (*hare*) von einem alltäglichen und befleckten (*ke*) trennt. Bei *chanoyu* beispielsweise, der Teezeremonie, gibt es einen rituellen Raum, der uns zum eigentlichen Teeraum hinführt, den *roji*-Teegarten. Der Teemeister Sen Rikyu lehrte, daß es unbedingt erforderlich sei, im Teegarten ein Gefühl der Demut (*suki*) zu erlangen, da die Teezeremonie eine »andere Welt« bilde, die sich außerhalb des alltäglichen Lebens befindet. In diese »andere Welt« geführt zu werden, bedeute, weltliche Angelegenheiten abzustreifen und in die Sphären des *mu* (Nichts) und des *ku*

magique et servant à marquer les limites d'un village et à éloigner les esprits sont tous *kekkai*. Ils indiquent clairement une ligne, une articulation qui détermine une fermeture. De là pouvons-nous imaginer les divisions *kekkai* comme des démarcations linéaires.

Néanmoins, une zone marginale est un espace non-A, non-B, qui n'appartient ni à A ni à B. En d'autres mots, elle est un espace sans rattachement, « détaché ». Et la signification de cet espace « détaché » s'éclaire dans le rite de passage qui détermine un domaine *hare* (pur) qui n'est pas de ce monde, hors du domaine *ke* (profane) de la vie quotidienne. Pour citer un exemple, dans la *chanoyu* (cérémonie du thé), nous trouvons un espace rituel qui nous guide vers la salle de thé. Le jardin de thé *roji* est ce type d'espace ; on le trouve toujours associé à la salle de thé. Le maître du thé Sen Rikyu enseignait qu'« il est essentiel de connaître le *suki* (humilité) dans le *roji* », car ce qui se passe à l'intérieur de la salle de thé constitue un « autre monde », différent de celui de la vie quotidienne. Etre introduit dans cet

yet there are still other visible and invisible factors that further reinforce spatial interrelationships: "suppositional kekkai", "conventional kekkai" and "taboo kekkai".

Japanese spatial articulations, certainly most of the kekkai devices we have already discussed, are premised to a greater or lesser extent upon the act of "supposing". The sanctuary roped off by the shimenawa is without a doubt a "suppositional kekkai" underwritten by pre-agreed assumptions. Indeed, when we start looking for culturally distinct signifiers, goza (straw mats), mosen (wool runner carpets), dohyo (raised earth rings), almost any area bounded by lines or surfaces can be considered "suppositional kekkai". A garden may be likened to an island, viewed as the mythical Chinese paradise of Mt. Penglai, and so on, to enjoy a heightened sense of creativity. The rule of thumb being that "suppositional" constructs always scale up, with mere points perceived as lines, and lines seen as planes. More unique to Japan, however, is the cultural tendency to "suppose" structures upon what is not present. Let us

(Leere) einzudringen. Das aber erfordere das »Passieren« einer »losgelösten« Randzone. Nicht zufällig hatte die ländlich geprägte Ästhetik der Teezeremonie das Ideal einer »Gebirgseinsiedelei in der Mitte der Stadt« angestrebt, also eines außerweltlichen Refugiums, obwohl weit weg in eine zeitlose Berglandschaft gedacht, inmitten des Stadtzentrums. Architektonisch besonders ausdrucksvoll ist die Randzone bei traditionellen japanischen Häusern im Bereich unter dem Dachvorsprung, dort, wo das Innere ins Äußere hinüberreicht. Hier befindet sich für gewöhnlich der engawa sowie die Stelle für das ritualisierte Ausziehen der Schuhe vor Betreten des Hauses, wie es in Japan üblich ist. Im alten Japan allerdings war dieser Vordach-Raum wesentlich offener und natürlicher angelegt, wobei das Ablegen der Schuhe ganz wörtlich das Abstreifen der bösen Geister bedeutete. Dieser Raum ist seinem Charakter nach eindeutig außerhalb des Hauses, strenggenommen jedoch »losgelöst«, gehört also weder dem inneren noch dem äußeren Bereich an.

« autre monde » signifie abandonner les préoccupations terrestres et atteindre la sphère du mu (rien) et du ku (vide). Et ceci entraîne le passage à travers une zone marginale. Il n'est pas sans signification que l'idéal auquel aspire l'esthétique rustique de la cérémonie du thé soit « un ermitage de montagne au cœur de la cité », c'est-à-dire un refuge de l'autre monde imaginé loin des collines éternelles et, cependant, exactement au centre de la ville. Cette zone marginale se trouve également revêtue d'une expression architecturalement soignée des maisons traditionnelles japonaises, sous les avant-toits, là où l'intérieur s'étend vers l'extérieur. C'est là que nous trouvons le plus généralement l'engawa et un endroit assez ritualisé pour le déchaussement qui précède l'entrée dans la maison, selon la coutume japonaise. Dans l'ancien Japon, cependant, ces espaces sous le toit étaient plus ouverts et proches de la nature, tandis que le déchaussement était un authentique rituel pour exorciser les forces maléfiques de l'extérieur. Cet espace est de caractère for-

Bamboo Hedge of Jisho-ji Temple (Ginkakuji Temple), Kyoto
Zaun aus Bambus beim Jisho-ji-Tempel (Ginkakuji-Tempel), Kyoto
Clôture de bambou du temple Jisho-ji (temple Ginkakuji), Kyoto

consider this *waka* verse by the late-12th-century poet Fujiwara Teika: "Casting wide my gaze / Neither flowers nor crimson leaves / From this bayside hovel of reeds / In the autumn twilight." One of the most famous selections from the Shinkokinshu anthology, it sings of sparseness and poverty, the "supposition" of what is not there giving rise to a contrast, the paradoxical absence of any substantial thing of beauty only adding more pathos to the scene.

Conventional *kekkai* and Taboo *kekkai*

Finally we come to "conventional *kekkai*" and "taboo *kekkai*". These are truly culturally specific. Even "*kekkai* devices" and "suppositional *kekkai*" such as we have examined are based upon systematised taboos and conventions. Nowhere are these formulaic systems ever clearly set forth. In this sense, "conventional *kekkai*" prove little more than hypothetical constructs founded upon tacit understandings, which might easily fall apart. Japanese culture must therefore

Das Empfinden für Randzonen hat auf die japanische Kultur und Kunst erheblichen Einfluß genommen. Ein Innenbereich, der bis in die Natur vordringt, ermöglicht ein tiefergehendes Gefühl der Verbundenheit mit der Umwelt, eine innigere Wertschätzung der Schönheit. Das »Manyoshu« wie auch andere Klassiker der japanischen Dichtkunst sind übervoll von Bekundungen der spirituellen Anmut eines Lebens mit der Natur.
So viel zu den Möglichkeiten der Abgrenzung von Räumen. Es gibt jedoch noch andere sichtbare und

unsichtbare Faktoren, mit Hilfe derer Raumbeziehungen verstärkt werden können: »angenommene *kekkai*«, »konventionelle *kekkai*« und »tabuisierte *kekkai*«.
Die japanischen Raumbestimmungen, gewiß der Großteil der von uns bisher besprochenen »instrumentellen *kekkai*«, hängen mehr oder weniger von »Annahmen« ab. Das durch das *shiménawa*-Seil abgeteilte Heiligtum gehört zweifellos zu den »angenommenen *kekkai*«, die von zuvor geschlossenen Vereinbarungen verbürgt werden.
Betrachten wir einige kulturspezi-

tement extérieur, mais, strictement parlant, il est « détaché », et n'appartient ni à l'intérieur ni à l'extérieur. Ce sens d'espace marginal a grandement contribué à la culture et à l'art japonais. L'intérieur qui se projette vers la nature permet une communion plus profonde avec l'environnement, une appréciation plus prolongée de la beauté. Témoins, le « Manyoshu » ainsi que les autres anciens récits poétiques classiques qui abondent en expressions sur la grâce spirituelle de la vie en communion avec la nature. Voici donc ce que l'on peut dire des

dispositifs qui divisent les espaces A et B. Il existe cependant d'autres facteurs visibles et invisibles qui peuvent encore renforcer davantage les relations spatiales : le « *kekkai* supposé », le « *kekkai* de convention », et le « *kekkai* tabou ».
Les articulations de l'espace japonais et, à coup sûr, la plupart des dispositifs *kekkai* que nous avons vus, sont voués à des extensions plus ou moins importantes en fonction du « supposé ». Le sanctuaire sans sa corde *shiménawa* est sans aucun doute un « *kekkai* supposé », soutenu par des croyances

incorporate an element of moderation lest it self-destruct as a cohesive entity. But since ancient times, moderation has prevailed over the social order directly through a pervasive status system, conversely elevated to an aesthetics of knowing one's place, the roots of which can be traced to the community, that is, to the "in-group out-group myths" held by the common people. Shared bonds within the community are a product of the socio-cultural mechanics of "exclusionism". By creating "others", a "we" comes into sharp relief. Deep down in

the regenerating, replicating life of the community we find such hidden mechanisms in the form of taboos directed at some object to be avoided. Overlaying these taboos are stories, folktales, and mountain lore. A typical song about a villager spirited away to an "other world" may thus convey the terrors of estrangement from the community, the underlying message being that no matter how tiresome the daily routine within the community, the world outside is unimaginably worse. Community bonding involves laying down a large number of taboos.

fische Bedeutungsträger – *goza* (Strohmatten), *mosen* (Wolläufer) oder *dohyo* (erhabene Erdwälle) –, werden wir sogar feststellen, daß fast jeder durch Linien oder Flächen begrenzte Bereich unter die »angenommenen *kekkai*« fällt. Ein Garten kann als eine Insel, diese wiederum als chinesisches Paradies am Berg Penglai angesehen werden und so weiter – ein Spiel sich steigernder Phantasie. Eine Regel dabei ist, daß sich die Annahmen stets erweitern, daß also Punkte als Linien wahrgenommen werden und Linien als Flächen. Spezifisch für die

Kultur Japans allerdings ist die Tendenz, Gebilde über etwas »anzunehmen«, das gar nicht anwesend ist. Schauen wir uns einen *waka*-Vers des Dichters Fujiwara Teika aus dem späten 12. Jahrhundert an: »Schweifend mein Blick/Weder Blumen noch purpurnes Laub/Von dieser Schilfhütte an der Bucht/Im herbstlichen Zwielicht.« Dieses Gedicht, eines der berühmtesten der »Shinkokinshu«-Anthologie, besingt Dürftigkeit und Armut; zur Erzeugung eines Kontrasts wird »angenommen«, was nicht da ist, wobei die paradoxe Abwesenheit aller

préalablement convenues. En effet, lorsque nous commençons à chercher des signifiants culturels distincts, presque chaque zone limitée par des lignes ou des surfaces peut être considérée comme un « *kekkai* supposé », par exemple le *goza* (petit tapis de paille), le *mosen* (tapis de laine courant), le *dohyo* (objet en terre dressé). Un jardin peut être comparé à une île, ou au paradis mythique chinois du mont Penglai etc., pour bénéficier d'un sens de créativité plus élevé. La règle étant que les constructions « supposées » sont toujours d'échelle

plus grande, avec de simples points perçus comme des lignes, et des lignes prenant valeur de plans. Plus typique du Japon, cependant, est la tendance culturelle à « supposer » des constructions sur ce qui n'est pas présent. Prenons ce poème *waka* du poète de la fin du XIIᵉ siècle, Fujiwara Teika, l'un des plus fameux extraits de l'anthologie Shinkokinshu : « Et je regarde les yeux grand ouverts/ni fleurs ni feuillage pourpre/autour de cette masure de roseaux au bord de la baie/dans la lumière crépusculaire de l'automne. » Ce poème célèbre la

Strangely enough then, at least by contemporary standards, peeping came to be fairly characteristic behaviour in Japan. Even so, people did not go stealing glances all the time; particular contexts governed when it was acceptable to peep. The issue here, as we have seen earlier, was that Japanese boundary markers such as *kekkai* devices can be physically ambiguous. Given the aim to compose a partition that interposes between spaces A and B yet allows them to communicate, it stands to reason that Japanese culture would be permissive about wandering eyes. Looking though such partitions ceased to be active peeking and became passive peeping – just happening to see. That much was permissible or unavoidable; anything else, of course, would be considered extremely rude. A very fine line draws both the spying party and the spied upon into a relationship of being permitted and permitting. It establishes certain mutual conventions of aesthetic: actually seeing what is "not seen", knowing what is "not there". Or perhaps "not knowing" what is there. Mutually exclusive

---

Schönheit der dargestellten Szene mehr Pathos verleiht.

Konventionelle *kekkai* und tabuisierte *kekkai*

Wenden wir uns schließlich den »konventionellen *kekkai*« sowie den »tabuisierten *kekkai*« zu; sie sind äußerst kulturspezifisch. Auch die vorher untersuchten »instrumentellen *kekkai*« und »angenommenen *kekkai*« beruhen auf systematisierten Tabus und Konventionen. Da eine eindeutige Definition dieser formelhaften Systeme jedoch nicht existiert, basieren »konventionelle *kekkai*« nur wenig mehr als hypothetische Konstrukte auf sehr labilen stillschweigenden Übereinkünften. Um sich in ihrem Zusammenhalt nicht selbst zu zerstören, muß die japanische Kultur ein regulatives Element integrieren. Seit der Antike dominiert dieses Regulativ die soziale Ordnung Japans, und zwar in Form eines alle Bereiche durchdringenden Statussystems, welches das Wissen um den eigenen gesellschaftlichen Rang zu einer Ästhetik erhoben hat. Das Verbindende innerhalb einer Gemeinschaft ist stets das Produkt soziokul-

---

rareté et la pauvreté, parle d'une « supposition » de ce qui manque pour créer un contraste, l'absence paradoxale de toute chose belle ajoutant encore un peu plus de pathos à la scène.

Kekkai de convention et *kekkai* tabou

Ces deux dernières formes de *kekkai* sont culturellement spécifiques. Même les « dispositifs *kekkai* » et les « *kekkai* supposés » que nous venons d'examiner reposent sur des tabous et des conventions systématisés. Nulle part ces systèmes formulés ne sont clairement expliqués. En ce sens, le « *kekkai* de convention » n'est guère plus qu'une construction hypothétique fondée sur une compréhension tacite, qui peut facilement s'effondrer. La culture japonaise doit par conséquent incorporer un élément de modération de peur qu'elle ne s'autodétruise en tant qu'unité cohérente. Mais depuis les temps anciens, la modération a directement prévalu dans l'ordre social, grâce à un subtil système de statut élevé à une esthétique de la place que chacun occupe,

propositions must be allowed to co-exist. This is a form of "suppositional *kekkai*". Such is the very complex character of the truly paradoxical relations, manners and other social constructs which have been codified into Japanese culture.

Consider, for instance, the ancient codes and customs surrounding *oshiidashi-ginu* or *uchiide no kinu* ornamented kimono sleeves. Heian period noblewomen, when riding in an ox carriage, would let a sleeve trail out below the split-reed blinds that supposedly concealed their person, thereby hinting at whoever was inside. "Conventional *kekkai*" at times serve to give spatial qualities to social status, so as to confer a mutually accorded space within the status system. This is never an actual space; no actual divisions break the continuum between upper and lower classes, or between men and women. It is far more the case that these are psychologically defined and consciously affected conventions. Still, the idea of substituting an abstract concept with a tangible spatial corollary is typically Japanese.

tureller Ausgrenzungsmechanismen. Durch die Schaffung von »Anderen« wird das »Wir« um so deutlicher umrissen. In den Tiefenschichten des sich regenerierenden und erhaltenden Lebens einer Gemeinschaft stoßen wir auf solche verborgenen Mechanismen als Tabus gegenüber bestimmten Objekten. Auf höherer Ebene kommen sie als Erzählungen und Märchen vor. Ein typisches Lied über einen Dorfbewohner, der in eine »andere Welt« gezaubert wird, transportiert daher die Schrecken der Entfremdung von der Gemeinschaft; ganz gleich, wie mühselig die alltägliche Arbeit auch sein mag, so lautet die Botschaft, die Welt außerhalb ist noch schrecklicher. Aus heutiger Sicht ist es erstaunlich, daß das gegenseitige Sich-Beobachten in Japan zu einem charakteristischen Verhalten werden konnte. Doch lagen die Menschen nicht allzeit auf der Lauer, um einen Blick zu erhaschen; gewisse Umstände bestimmten, wann das Beobachten als annehmbar galt. Wir haben bereits festgestellt, daß japanische Grenzmarkierungen wie die »instrumentellen *kekkai*« eine materielle Ambiguität

et dont les racines remontent à la communauté, c'est-à-dire, aux mythes « intérieur au groupe » *versus* « extérieur au groupe », intégrés par les gens du peuple. Les liens partagés à l'intérieur de la communauté sont le produit d'un mécanisme socio-culturel d'exclusion. La création des « autres » fait fortement ressortir le « nous ». Nous trouvons de tels mécanismes cachés sous forme de tabous dirigés vers certaines choses à éviter, profondément enracinés dans la vie auto-régénérée et répétitive de la communauté. Au-dessus de ces tabous figurent des histoires, des récits populaires et les connaissances de la vie de la montagne. Une chanson typique, composée sur un villageois disparu vers « un autre monde », véhiculera ainsi les terreurs de la mise à l'écart de la communauté, le message sousjacent étant qu'aussi fastidieuse la routine à l'intérieur de la communauté puisse-t-elle être, le monde extérieur est incroyablement pire. Les liens qui se forment dans la communauté impliquent la création d'un grand nombre de tabous.

Ainsi est-il étrange, du moins au

Native Cosmology and Western Culture

For the sake of argument, I have categorised three different types of *kekkai* constructs, which however appropriate, do not necessarily cover the whole of Japanese spatial awareness. They are merely general parameters. Let me stress that these various constructs never interrelate in any simple manner, but overlap in truly strange and complex ways to create the polysemous character of Japanese architectural space.

The point of emphasizing what I have called *kekkai* constructs is that native Japanese spatial concepts are still alive in Japanese society today. Thus I have explained something of Japan's culture of *kekkai* constructs, when actually they go back to a more fundamentally human level. Draw a line on the floor and there we have a partitioned or even an enclosed area. The same holds for surrounding an area with posts.

These means of establishing boundaries transcend the particular cultural properties of any one people. Or to take the discussion further, even

Takiginoh (Noh dance performed outdoors) at Kofukuji Temple, Nara

Takiginoh (Aufführung eines Noh-Tanzes im Freien) vor dem Kofukuji-Tempel, Nara

Takiginoh (danse Noh, qui se donne à l'extérieur) au temple Kofukuji, Nara

---

aufweisen können. Da ihr Zweck zwar die Aufteilung in zwei Räume A und B ist, dabei aber die Kommunikationsfähigkeit zwischen beiden erhalten bleiben soll, folgt es einer gewissen Logik, daß die japanische Kultur sich gelegentlichen Blicken gegenüber nicht verschließt. Der Blick durch solche Raumteiler hindurch war demnach nicht länger ein aktives »Beobachten«, sondern ein passives – ein beiläufiges Mitansehen. Das war tolerierbar oder unvermeidlich; alles darüber Hinausgehende hätte als äußerst grob gegolten. Eine sehr feine Linie

trennt zwischen dem Beobachter und dem Beobachteten und schafft eine Beziehung von Geduldetem und Dulder. In der Folge entstehen gewisse ästhetische Konventionen, die für beide gelten: das Sehen dessen, was »nicht gesehen« wird, das Wissen um das, was »nicht da« ist. Oder auch das »Unwissen« von dem, was vorhanden ist. Einander ausschließenden Aussagen muß die Erlaubnis zur Koexistenz erteilt werden. Das ist eine Spielart der »angenommenen *kekkai*«, ein Teil der paradoxen Beziehungen und Umgangsformen sowie anderer sozia-

---

regard de nos critères contemporains, que le voyeurisme soit devenu un comportement japonais assez caractéristique. Mais même dans ce cas, il ne s'agissait pas de regarder tout le temps, il fallait un contexte particulier pour que l'action de regarder soit acceptée. Notre argument ici, comme nous l'avons vu plus haut, est qu'au Japon, les marqueurs des limites, comme les « dispositifs *kekkai* », peuvent être physiquement ambigus. Etant donné l'objectif d'élever une séparation entre les espaces A et B, tout en leur permettant de communi-

quer encore, il semble raisonnable que la culture japonaise accepte les regards errants. Regarder à travers ces séparations cessait ainsi d'être un voyeurisme actif pour devenir passif, confondu avec la simple vision. Ce regard-là était permis et inévitable, mais tout autre aurait été considéré, bien entendu, comme extrêmement impoli. Une ligne de séparation très ténue court entre celui qui espionne et l'espionné dans une relation entre le permis et l'interdit. Elle établit certaines conventions mutuelles esthétiques : voir réellement ce qui n'est

those "conventional *kekkai*" seemingly already gone from contemporary life have not in fact disappeared, but only slipped down into the underlying Japanese cosmology.

Ever since the Meiji Restoration in 1868, we Japanese have striven to achieve a modern Westernised society, learning in the process that "culture is never lost". Many lament the loss of Japanese traditions. Indeed, in actual fact, modernisation has dismantled many different national cultures and cosmologies, not just Japan's. Yet when discussing culture, it is more useful to look at all that was "not lost" in spite of the Westernisation policies of the Meiji regime. Naturally, I do not mean to say that all aspects survived modernisation. The demise of traditional politics and community bring new changes to the social order. Yet even a political environment must draw upon native cosmological premises. The real issue here is whether, in our transition from pre-Meiji to modern life, we ever really prepared ourselves for the change or gave proper ceremony to that rebirth. Did we undergo any kind of initi-

ler Komponenten, die in den Kodex der japanischen Kultur eingeflossen sind.

Denken wir etwa an die alten Verhaltenskodizes und Bräuche um *oshiidashi-ginu* oder *ushiidé no kinu*, die mit Ornamenten verzierten Ärmel des Kimonos. Die Edelfrauen der Heian-Periode ließen, wenn sie in einer von Ochsen gezogenen Kutsche reisten, einen Ärmel aus der Schilfblende hängen, die ihre Identität angeblich verbergen sollte, und gaben somit preis, wer sich im Inneren befand. »Konventionelle *kekkai*« dienen gelegentlich dazu, dem sozialen Status auch zu einer räumlichen Qualität zu verhelfen, so als würden sie ihm einen gemeinhin anerkannten Raum innerhalb des Statussystems zuteilen. Dabei handelt es sich niemals um wirkliche Räume; keine tatsächlichen Schranken unterteilen das Kontinuum zwischen den oberen und den unteren Klassen oder zwischen Mann und Frau. Vielmehr sind es psychologisch bestimmte und im Bewußtsein eingehaltene Konventionen. Doch auch die Ersetzung eines abstrakten Begriffs durch eine greifbar-materielle Raum-

« pas vu », savoir ce qui n'est « pas là » ; ou peut-être « ne pas savoir » ce qui est là. On permet à des propositions qui s'excluent de coexister. C'est une forme de « *kekkai* supposé ». Telles sont les relations, manières d'être, et autres constructions sociales authentiquement paradoxales codifiées de la culture japonaise. Considérons, un instant, les anciens codes et coutumes entourant l'*oshiidashi-ginu* ou *uchiidé no kinu* des manches ornementées des kimonos. Les femmes nobles de la période Heian transportées dans une charrette à bœufs laissaient dépasser un bout de leur manche entre les claustras de bambous fendus supposés dissimuler leur personne, faisant ainsi comprendre qui était à l'intérieur. Le « *kekkai* de convention » à certains moments sert à attribuer des qualités spatiales au statut social, afin de générer un espace mutuellement reconnu à l'intérieur du système de statut. Il ne s'agit jamais d'un espace réel, aucune division ne rompt le *continuum* entre les classes supérieures et inférieures, ou entre les hommes et les femmes. Il s'agit plutôt de conventions se définissant psychologique-

ation? The answer is no. And for that reason, our present lifestyle is in confusion.

We have now reached a point where we must judge things unemotionally. We are living in the modern world. Furthermore, we live in a world of electronic media. But it is also true that we still live in the same real space that is Japan. Modernisation may have been inevitable, but can one maintain that Westernisation ultimately suited Japan's own cultural cosmology? Was any attempt made to make it more suitable? As I see it, much of Japanese culture is an accumulation of elements either symbiotically acculturated or accepted as they are, without question, from abroad. In which case, the task at hand would now seem to be to check how this biomass of Western culture is being digested in the Japanese cultural tract.

Either way, even with the one-dimensionality that modern rationalism brought to maturity in today's information-oriented society, in which global social, cultural and political newsbites race around the world in real-time, I do not feel that the world

abfolge ist typisch für die japanische Kultur.

Traditionelles Weltbild und westliche Kultur

Zur Vereinfachung habe ich zwischen drei Kategorien von *kekkai*-Konstrukten unterschieden, die zwar nicht alle Aspekte des japanischen Raumbbewußtseins abdecken, aber allgemeine Parameter darstellen. Ich möchte betonen, daß die verschiedenen Konstrukte niemals völlig eindeutig zueinander in Beziehung stehen; vielmehr überlappen sie sich auf sehr eigenartige und komplexe Weise, was zu dem mehrdeutigen Charakter des architektonischen Raums in Japan führt.

Ich lege soviel Wert auf die *kekkai*-Konstrukte, da diese traditionellen Raumauffassungen auch in der heutigen japanischen Gesellschaft noch lebendig sind. Der abstrakte Begriff *kekkai*, den ich zu erklären versucht habe, läßt sich aber auf eine einfachere, menschliche Ebene bringen. Zieht man auf dem Boden eine Linie, so verfügt man bereits über einen abgegrenzten oder gar eingeschlossenen Raum. Das gleiche gilt für einen

ment, et consciemment affectées. L'idée de substituer un concept abstrait à un corollaire spatial tangible est typiquement japonaise.

Cosmologie indigène et culture occidentale

Pour ma démonstration, j'ai classé les constructions *kekkai* en trois types différents, classification qui, même si elle est appropriée, ne couvre pas nécessairement la totalité du champ de la conscience japonaise de l'espace. Ils représentent tout au plus des paramètres généraux. Il me reste à montrer que ces constructions diverses ne sont en aucune façon reliées entre elles par des relations simples, mais qu'elles se recouvrent de manière complexe et très étrange pour donner naissance au caractère polysémique de l'espace architectural japonais.

L'intérêt de ce que j'ai appelé les constructions *kekkai* est que les concepts indigènes spatiaux japonais sont toujours bien vivants dans la culture du Japon d'aujourd'hui. De cette manière, j'ai tenté d'expliquer la culture japonaise des constructions *kekkai*, qui remontent en fait à un

will or can be dominated by a single reductionist logic. I sincerely believe that each different cultural sphere will eventually rediscover its own distinct time and space, while timely new methods will come to transcend this one-dimensionality.

What is important today, then, is whether or not timely methods can develop from here on. Here, in addressing the subject of *kekkai* constructs, my motive has been to consider whether these traditional Japanese spatial concepts might serve as bases for the creation of still newer, more timely methods. Naturally, I do not expect any sudden solutions. Nonetheless, when considering ideas for the future, I believe a "recycling of cultural memories" is a good place to start.

---

durch Pfosten abgesteckten Bereich. Diese Mittel der Grenzziehung sind allen Völkern und Kulturen geläufig. So sind auch die »konventionellen *kekkai*«, die bereits aus unserem täglichen Leben verschwunden zu sein scheinen, in Wirklichkeit gar nicht verloren, sondern lediglich in das ihnen zugrundeliegende japanische Weltbild eingegangen.

Seit der Restauration der Meidschi-Epoche 1868 haben wir Japaner unablässig danach gestrebt, eine moderne Gesellschaft westlichen Vorbilds zu werden, und dabei gelernt, daß eine »Kultur niemals ganz verlorengeht«. Zwar beklagen viele den Verlust japanischer Traditionen, und tatsächlich sind durch die Modernisierung viele verschiedene Nationalkulturen und Weltbilder zerstört worden, nicht nur das japanische. Doch würde uns diese Diskussion mehr eintragen, wenn wir uns auf das konzentrieren würden, was dabei trotzdem »nicht verlorenging«. Selbstverständlich will ich damit nicht behaupten, daß alle kulturellen Aspekte die Modernisierung überdauern konnten. Der Untergang einer überkommenen Politik

---

niveau humain encore plus fondamental. Tirez une ligne sur le sol et vous avez un espace divisé, voire même enclos. Il en va de même pour un espace marqué par des poteaux. Ces moyens d'établir des frontières transcendent les propriétés culturelles particulières de tout peuple. Ou, pour aller plus loin, même les « *kekkai* de convention » qui semblent ne plus être présents dans la vie contemporaine, n'ont en réalité pas disparu mais se sont tout simplement coulés dans la cosmologie japonaise sous-jacente.

Depuis la restauration Meiji de 1868, nous, les Japonais, nous sommes efforcés de mettre en place une société occidentalisée moderne, et avons appris dans le même temps que « la culture ne se perd jamais. » Beaucoup se lamentent sur la perte des traditions japonaises. En fait, la modernisation a démantelé de nombreuses cultures et cosmologies nationales, et pas seulement celles du Japon. Dans ce discours culturel, il vaut mieux considérer tout ce qui n'a pas été perdu, en dépit de la politique d'occidentalisation du Meiji. Naturellement,

und Gesellschaftsform führt immer zu neuen Entwicklungen innerhalb der sozialen Ordnung. Doch jedes politische System muß auf bestimmte Prämissen des traditionellen Weltbildes Rücksicht nehmen. Die sich hier stellende Frage ist doch, ob wir uns beim Übergang von der Vor-Meidschi-Epoche zum modernen Lebensstil jemals wirklich auf die damit einhergehenden Veränderungen eingestellt haben. Durchlebten wir irgendeine Art von Initiation? Die Antwort ist eindeutig negativ. Und aus diesem Grund ist unser augenblicklicher Lebensstil auch so konfus.

Wir haben einen Punkt erreicht, an dem wir die Dinge emotionslos betrachten müssen. Wir leben in einer modernen Welt, einer Welt elektronischer Medien. Trotz alledem leben wir in Japan. Die Modernisierung mag unvermeidbar gewesen sein, doch paßte die Verwestlichung tatsächlich zu der spezifischen Kultur Japans? Wurde irgend etwas unternommen, die westliche Kultur der japanischen anzupassen? In meinen Augen besteht ein Großteil der heutigen japanischen

je ne veux pas dire que tous ces aspects ont survécu à la modernisation. La fin des politiques et des communautés traditionnelles apporte son lot de changements à l'ordre social. Mais même un environnement politique doit se nourrir des prémisses cosmologiques indigènes. L'objectif, ici, est de savoir si dans notre transition de la période pré-Meiji au style de vie moderne, nous nous sommes vraiment bien préparés au changement inhérent, et si nous avons fait ce qu'il fallait pour saluer cette nouvelle naissance. Sommes-nous passés par un quelconque rite d'initiation ? La réponse est négative. Et c'est la raison pour laquelle nos modes de vie actuels sont en pleine confusion. Nous avons maintenant atteint un point où nous devons juger les choses sans émotion. Nous vivons dans le monde moderne. Nous vivons de plus dans un monde de médias électroniques. Mais il est également vrai que nous vivons toujours dans le même espace réel, qui est celui du Japon. La modernisation a peut-être été inévitable, mais l'occidentalisation était-elle, ultimement, adaptée à notre

Kultur aus einer Akkumulation von Einflüssen, die entweder symbiotisch assimiliert oder aber unverändert von außen übernommen worden sind, ohne sie zu hinterfragen. Wobei zu überprüfen wäre, wie die westliche Biomasse von den kulturellen Eingeweiden Japans verdaut werden kann. Sogar angesichts der Eindimensionalität, die der moderne Rationalismus in unserer heutigen Informationsgesellschaft zur vollen Blüte entfalten konnte, in der global erfaßte kulturelle, soziale und politische Infohäppchen blitzschnell um die Erde rotieren, glaube ich nicht, daß die Welt von einer einzigen reduktionistischen Logik dominiert werden kann. Ich bin davon überzeugt, daß jede Kultur ihre besonderen Zeit- und Raumvorstellungen wiederentdecken wird und daß neue zeitgemäße Methoden zur Überwindung der Eindimensionalität entwickelt werden. Worauf es heute also ankommt, ist herauszufinden, ob solche Methoden eine Chance haben. So war auch meine Untersuchung von *kekkai*-Konstrukten von der Frage geleitet, ob die traditionellen japanischen Auffassun-

propre cosmologie ? Avons-nous essayé de rendre cette adaptation plus aisée ? A mon sens, une grande partie de la culture japonaise est une accumulation d'éléments symbiotiquement acculturés ou acceptés de l'étranger comme ils sont, sans questionnement. Dans ce cas, la tâche actuelle est peut-être bien de vérifier comment cette biomasse de culture occidentale peut être digérée dans le champ culturel japonais.

De toute façon, même avec l'unidimensionnalité que le rationalisme moderne a porté à maturité dans la société d'aujourd'hui, orientée vers l'information, et dans laquelle les nouveautés sociales, culturelles et politiques tournent autour du monde en temps réel, je ne vois pas comment les différentes sphères culturelles pourraient éventuellement retrouver leur propre temps, leur propre espace, alors que de nouveaux moyens de transcender cette unidimensionnalité font leur apparition.

Ce qui est important aujourd'hui, c'est de savoir si des méthodes opportunes peuvent être mises au point ou non. En abordant le sujet de ces

gen von Raum als Grundlage für die Entwicklung neuer, zeitgemäßerer Methoden dienen könnten. Natürlich erwarte ich keine sofortigen Lösungen. Doch scheint mir bei der Erwägung von Ideen für die Zukunft ein »Recycling des kulturellen Gedächtnisses« ein guter Ausgangspunkt zu sein.

constructions *kekkai*, mon motif était de voir si les concepts japonais traditionnels de l'espace pouvaient servir de base à la création de méthodes plus nouvelles et plus opportunes. Naturellement, je ne m'attends pas à des solutions rapides. Néanmoins, lorsque l'on considère les idées valables pour le futur, je crois qu'un « recyclage des mémoires culturelles » est un bon point de départ.

Main Entrance of Jisho-ji Temple (Ginkakuji Temple), Kyoto
Haupteingang des Jisho-ji-Tempels (Ginkakuji-Tempel), Kyoto
Entrée principale du temple Jisho-ji (temple Ginkakuji), Kyoto

BIBLIOGRAPHY

AKASAKA, Norio/"Ijinronjosetsu"/1985/Sunagoyashobo/Tokyo
AMINO, Yoshihiko/"Muen Kugai Raku"/1978/Heibonsha/Tokyo
BOLLNOW, Otto Friedrich/"Mensch und Raum"/1994/Kohlhammer/Stuttgart
ELIADE, Mircea/"A History of Religious Ideas"/1978/The University of Chicago Press/Chicago
ELIADE, Mircea/"Images and Symbols"/1991/Princeton University Press/Princeton
HIDA, Norio/"Sakuteiki-kara-mita-Zoen" [SD sensho 193]/1985/Kajima Shuppankai/Tokyo
HORIGUCHI, Sutemi/"Rikyu-no-Chashitsu"/1977/Kajima Kenkyujo Shuppankai/Tokyo
INOUE, Mitsuo/"Nihonkenchiku-no-Kukan" [SD sensho 37]/1969/Kajima Shuppankai/Tokyo
ITO, Teiji/"Nihon-Dezain-Ron" [SD sensho 5]/1966/Kajima Shuppankai/Tokyo
KUBOTA, Jun/"Yugen-to-Sonoshuhen" [Koza Nihon-Shiso Vol. 5]/1984/Tokyo Daigaku Shuppankai/Tokyo
MATSUOKA, Seigo/"Kachofugetsu-no-Kagaku"/1994/The Tanko-Shinsha Co./Kyoto
MORI, Osamu/"Teien"/1988/Tokyodo Shuppan/Tokyo
MURAI, Yasuhiko/"Sennorikyu–Sonoshogai-to-Chanoyu-no-Imi"/1971/Nihon Hoso Shuppan Kyokai/Tokyo
NAKAMURA, Masao (Editorial Supervisor)/"Chashitsu-to-Roji" [Sukiya-Kenchiku-Shusei]/1979/Shogakukan/Tokyo
TARUMI, Minoru/"Kekkai-no-Kozo"/1990/Meicho Shuppan/Tokyo
SEN, Soshitsu/MURATA, Jiro/KITAMURA, Denbe/"CHASHITSU The Original Drawings and Photographic Illustrations of the Typical Japanese Tea Architectures and Gardens"/1959/The Tanko-Shinsha Co./Kyoto
"Girei-to-Seimeigenri" [Quarterly: Shizen-to-Bunka Summer #37]/1992/Nihon National Trust/Tokyo
"Shoshuraku-no-Chimei" [Quarterly: Shizen-to-Bunka Summer #41]/1993/Nihon National Trust/Tokyo
"Chashitsu-wo-Yomu" [Nagomi June]/1991/The Tanko-Shinsha Co./Kyoto
"Shikiri-no-Sign" [Nagomi May]/1992/The Tanko-Shinsha Co./Kyoto

BIBLIOGRAPHIE

AKASAKA, Norio/»Ijinronjosetsu«/1985/Sunagoyashobo/Tokio
AMINO, Yoshihiko/»Muen Kugai Raku«/1978/Heibonsha/Tokio
BOLLNOW, Otto Friedrich/»Mensch und Raum«/1994/Kohlhammer/Stuttgart
ELIADE, Mircea/»Geschichte der religiösen Ideen«/1987/Herder/Frankfurt
ELIADE, Mircea/»Ewige Bilder und Sinnbilder«/1988/Insel/Frankfurt
HIDA, Norio/»Sakuteiki-kara-mita-Zoen« [SD sensho 193]/1985/Kajima Shuppankai/Tokio
HORIGUCHI, Sutemi/»Rikyu-no-Chashitsu«/1977/Kajima Kenkyujo Shuppankai/Tokio
INOUE, Mitsuo/»Nihonkenchiku-no-Kukan« [SD sensho 37]/1969/Kajima Shuppankai/Tokio
ITO, Teiji/»Nihon-Dezain-Ron« [SD sensho 5]/1966/Kajima Shuppankai/Tokio
KUBOTA, Jun/»Yugen-to-Sonoshuhen« [Koza Nihon-Shiso Bd. 5]/1984/Tokio Daigaku Shuppankai/Tokio
MATSUOKA, Seigo/»Kachofugetsu-no-Kagaku«/1994/The Tanko-Shinsha Co./Kyoto
MORI, Osamu/»Teien«/1988/Tokyodo Shuppan/Tokio
MURAI, Yasuhiko/»Sennorikyu–Sonoshogai-to-Chanoyu-no-Imi«/1971/Nihon Hoso Shuppan Kyokai/Tokio
NAKAMURA, Masao (Herausgeber)/»Chashitsu-to-Roji« [Sukiya-Kenchiku-Shusei]/1979/Shogakukan/Tokio
TARUMI, Minoru/»Kekkai-no-Kozo«/1990/Meicho Shuppan/Tokio
SEN, Soshitsu/MURATA, Jiro/KITAMURA, Denbe/»CHASHITSU The Original Drawings and Photographic Illustrations of the Typical Japanese Tea Architectures and Gardens«/1959/The Tanko-Shinsha Co./Kyoto
»Girei-to-Seimeigenri« [Vierteljahresschrift: Shizen-to-Bunka Summer #37]/1992/Nihon National Trust/Tokio
»Shoshuraku-no-Chimei« [Vierteljahresschrift: Shizen-to-Bunka Summer #41]/1993/Nihon National Trust/Tokio
»Chashitsu-wo-Yomu« [Nagomi June]/1991/The Tanko-Shinsha Co./Kyoto
»Shikiri-no-Sign« [Nagomi May]/1992/The Tanko-Shinsha Co./Kyoto

BIBLIOGRAPHIE

AKASAKA, Norio/« Ijinronjosetsu »/1985/Sunagoyashobo/Tokyo
AMINO, Yoshihiko/« Muen Kugai Raku »/1978/Heibonsha/Tokyo
BOLLNOW, Otto Friedrich/« Mensch und Raum »/1994/Kohlhammer/Stuttgart
ELIADE, Mircea/« Traité d'Histoire des Religions »/1989/Payot/Paris
ELIADE, Mircea/« Images et Symboles »/1979/Gallimard/Paris
HIDA, Norio/« Sakuteiki-kara-mita-Zoen » [SD sensho 193]/1985/Kajima Shuppankai/Tokyo
HORIGUCHI, Sutemi/« Rikyu-no-Chashitsu »/1977/Kajima Kenkyujo Shuppankai/Tokyo
INOUE, Mitsuo/« Nihonkenchiku-no-Kukan » [SD sensho 37]/1969/Kajima Shuppankai/Tokyo
ITO, Teiji/« Nihon-Dezain-Ron » [SD sensho 5]/1966/Kajima Shuppankai/Tokyo
KUBOTA, Jun/« Yugen-to-Sonoshuhen » [Koza Nihon-Shiso Vol. 5]/1984/Tokyo Daigaku Shuppankai/Tokyo
MATSUOKA, Seigo/« Kachofugetsu-no-Kagaku »/1994/The Tanko-Shinsha Co./Kyoto
MORI, Osamu/« Teien »/1988/Tokyodo Shuppan/Tokyo
MURAI, Yasuhiko/« Sennorikyu–Sonoshogai-to-Chanoyu-to-Imi »/1971/Nihon Hoso Shuppan Kyokai/Tokyo
NAKAMURA, Masao (Edition supervisée par)/« Chashitsu-to-Roji » [Sukiya-Kenchiku-Shusei]/1979/Shogakukan/Tokyo
TARUMI, Minoru/« Kekkai-no-Kozo »/1990/Meicho Shuppan/Tokyo
SEN, Soshitsu/MURATA, Jiro/KITAMURA, Denbe/« CHASHITSU The Original Drawings and Photographic Illustrations of the Typical Japanese Tea Architectures and Gardens »/1959/The Tanko-Shinsha Co./Kyoto
« Girei-to-Seimeigenri » [Trimestriel: Shizen-to-Bunka Summer #37]/1992/Nihon National Trust/Tokyo
« Shoshuraku-no-Chimei » [Trimestriel: Shizen-to-Bunka Summer #41]/1993/Nihon National Trust/Tokyo
« Chashitsu-wo-Yomu » [Nagomi June]/1991/The Tanko-Shinsha Co./Kyoto
« Shikiri-no-Sign » [Nagomi May]/1992/The Tanko-Shinsha Co./Kyoto

JI-AN
Tea-Room
1993

JI-AN, GYO-AN, SO-AN
Tea-Room
1993

Toward a New Tea-Room

Shigeru Uchida

A tea-room is an architectural setting for the tea-ceremony. But what is the tea-ceremony? This question seems easy, yet it is extremely difficult. The literal meaning of the tea-ceremony is to have a festivity, inviting guests and serving tea. But the behavioural idea behind inviting guests for tea is not so easily understood. The principle of the tea-ceremony is often said to be contained in the term *ichigo ichie*: one meets another only once in a life-time. Therefore, one must do one's best to appreciate the meeting. Inviting guests is an important occasion in

Für einen neuen Teeraum

Shigeru Uchida

Der Teeraum bildet den architektonischen Rahmen einer Teezeremonie. Doch was genau ist eine Teezeremonie? Die Frage erscheint einfach, ist aber äußerst schwierig zu beantworten. Wörtlich ist damit das Veranstalten einer Festlichkeit gemeint, bei der den eingeladenen Gästen Tee serviert wird. Der sich dahinter verbergende Verhaltenskodex ist hingegen nicht so leicht zu verstehen. Das Prinzip der Teezeremonie wird häufig durch die Worte *ichigo ichie* ausgedrückt: Man trifft einander nur einmal im Leben. Deshalb muß man sein

Vers une nouvelle salle de thé

Shigeru Uchida

Une salle de thé est un cadre architectural pour la cérémonie du thé. Mais qu'est-ce que la cérémonie du thé ? Cette question semble facile, bien qu'elle soit extrêmement délicate. La signification littérale est de tenir une fête, d'inviter des amis et de servir du thé. Mais le comportement qui régit l'invitation d'hôtes pour le thé n'est pas si facile à comprendre. On dit souvent que le principe de la cérémonie du thé est contenu dans le terme *ichigo ichie* : on ne rencontre l'autre qu'une fois dans sa vie. Aussi doit-on faire de son mieux pour

this once-in-a-lifetime sense. The host and guests must try to attain a profound exchange of ideas.

Rikyu (one of the great tea-masters of the 16th century) claimed that tea is there to cure one's thirst. His words may sound extremely simple, but the thirst he mentions refers to the thirst of one's soul and to the thirst present in relationships. For the way of tea, relationships possess quite significant meanings.

Zen philosophy advocates that we are born and destined to die within the broad providence of the universe, within relationships among men, objects, nature and the universe. The world of tea surpasses the ordinary, physical realm, and the participants' minds are unconsciously led onward to the realm of supernatural necessity. The Zen monk Ikkyu of the 15th century explains that the aim of tea and Zen are the same. A tea-room is a space and a distinct architectural environment, and its true form appears with the act of the tea-ceremony. Yet, a tea-room is not a fixed aesthetic world, it is conceived of far more as space that reflects the spirit of the tea-ceremony and the philosophy of a host's entertainment.

Bestes geben, um diese Begegnung angemessen zu würdigen. Das Einladen von Gästen wird vor dem Hintergrund dieser Einmaligkeit zu einem bedeutenden Ereignis. Gastgeber und Gäste müssen daher versuchen, einen intensiven Gedankenaustausch zu erlangen.

Von Rikyu, einem der großen Teemeister des 16. Jahrhunderts, stammt der Ausspruch, daß der Tee zum Löschen des Durstes diene. Seine Worte mögen einfältig klingen, doch der Durst verweist hier auf den Durst unserer Seele, auf den Durst, der sich in zwischenmenschlichen Beziehungen äußert. Bei der Teezeremonie kommt diesen Beziehungen eine große Bedeutung zu.

Die Zen-Philosophie setzt unsere Geburt und unseren Tod in den Zusammenhang einer universalen Vorsehung, in das Beziehungsgeflecht zwischen den Menschen, den Dingen, der Natur und dem Universum. Die Teezeremonie geht über das Gewöhnlich-Dinghafte hinaus, wobei die Teilnehmer unbewußt übernatürlichen Erfordernissen entgegengeführt werden. Der im 15. Jahrhundert lebende Zen-Mönch Ikkyu erklärt, daß die Absichten der Teezeremonie und des Zen identisch seien. Ein Teeraum ist ein Raum mit einer genau festgelegten architektonischen Formensprache, seine wahre Gestalt offenbart sich allerdings erst im Verlauf der Teezeremonie. In diesem Sinn folgt der Teeraum keiner festgeschriebenen Ästhetik, sondern bietet sich vielmehr als ein Raum dar, welcher den Geist der Teezeremonie und die der Unterhaltung des Gastgebers zugrundeliegende Philosophie widerspiegelt.

apprécier cette rencontre. Inviter des hôtes est une occasion importante dans ce sens du « une fois dans la vie ». L'invitant et les invités doivent tenter d'échanger leurs idées de façon profonde.

Rikyu (un des grands maîtres du thé au XVIe siècle) assurait que le thé servait à étancher la soif. Ses paroles peuvent paraître simples, mais la soif se réfère à celle de l'autre, et à celle que l'on trouve dans le besoin de relations avec les autres. A travers le thé, les relations revêtent des sens importants.

La philosophie Zen nous dit que nous sommes nés et destinés à mourir à l'intérieur d'une large présence de l'univers, dans le cadre de relations entre les hommes, les choses, la nature et l'univers. Le monde du thé dépasse le champ ordinaire et physique, et les esprits des participants à la cérémonie sont inconsciemment orientés vers l'univers de la nécessité surnaturelle. Le moine zen Ikkyu (XVe siècle), explique que le but du thé et du zen sont les mêmes. Une salle de thé est un espace et un environnement architectural distinct, et sa vraie forme se révèle dans l'acte de la cérémonie du thé. A cet égard, une salle de thé n'est pas un monde esthétique en soi, mais plutôt un espace qui reflète l'esprit de la cérémonie du thé et la philosophie de la réception de l'hôte.

GYO-AN
Tea-Room
1993

SO-AN
Tea-Room
1993

AOYAMA-MIHONCHO
Paper Showroom
Shibuya, Tokyo
1989

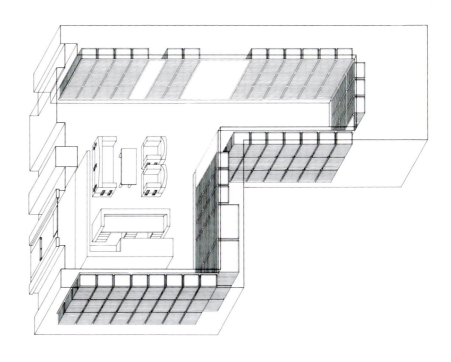

ITCHOH
Restaurant
Aoyama, Tokyo
1988

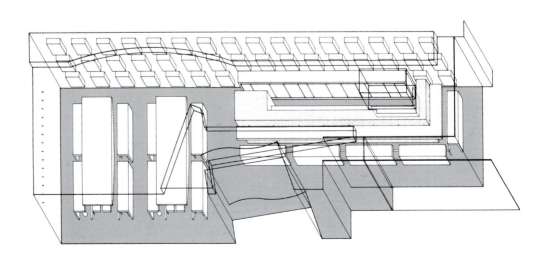

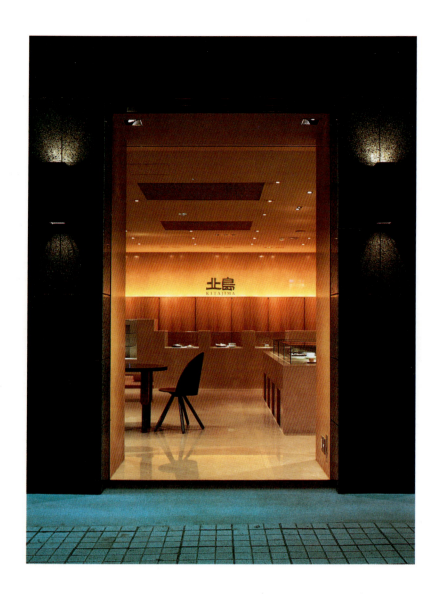

KITAJIMA
Confectionery
Saga
1990

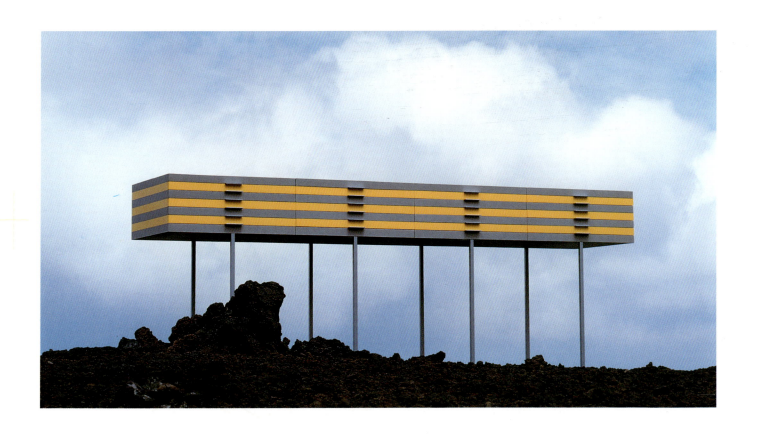

HORIZONTAL
Cabinet
1992

VERTICAL Series
Cabinet
1992

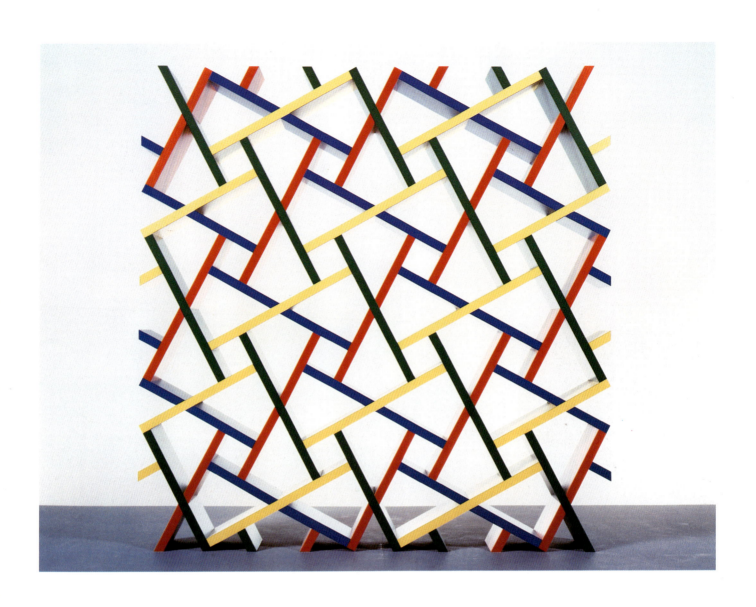

STORMY WEATHER
Shelf
1991

EAST OF THE SUN
Table
1992

Design and Everyday Life
Shigeru Uchida

When we look at Japanese design magazines, we find that many designs are of boutiques. This is a trend that has been on the rise since 1975 and is even becoming the mainstream of interior designing. What is the reason behind this trend?

It was back in the 70s that interior design became a focal point in Japan, and the lifestyle in Japan has drastically changed since then. However, the truth is that the phenomenon actually budded in the 60s. The 60s marked a period of transformation in the developed countries.

Design und Alltagsleben
Shigeru Uchida

Beim Blick in japanische Designzeitschriften fällt die große Anzahl von Entwürfen für Boutiquen auf. Dieser Trend hat sich seit 1975 zunehmend verstärkt und ist inzwischen zu einem Hauptbetätigungsfeld für Innenarchitekten geworden. Was sind die Hintergründe dieser Entwicklung?

In den 70er Jahren wandte man sich in Japan mit großer Aufmerksamkeit der Innenarchitektur zu, und seitdem hat sich der Lebensstil radikal verändert. Die Ursprünge dieses Phänomens müssen aber bereits in den 60er Jahren gesucht werden, die den

Design et vie quotidienne
Shigeru Uchida

Quand nous feuilletons les magazines de design japonais, nous trouvons de nombreux articles sur des boutiques. C'est une tendance en pleine croissance depuis 1975 et qui tend même à devenir le courant principal de l'architecture intérieure. Quelle est la raison cachée de cette évolution ?

C'est au cours des années 70 que l'architecture intérieure devient un des grands centres d'intérêt des Japonais, et le style de vie a considérablement changé au Japon depuis cette date. Cependant, la vérité est que ce phénomène était né dès les années

Significant discrepancies and imbalances in modern society became apparent. As Lewis Mumford noted, "modern society is characterized by power, mass production, standardization, systemization, regulation and unification." This was a description of a society that aimed at materialistic satiation, and that was supported by both science and technology. However, such a society must ultimately challenge any belief in individual uniqueness. The crucial issue for the developed countries was that their societies were strongly regulated and thus did not even possess an incentive for change.

The purpose of design in everyday life is to support the life of real people. This function focuses on the "soul", which has recently been highlighted in various facets. And this very focus was already present in the 60s.

The 70s were a period of change in which problems that were recognised to exist between people, society and the natural environment were addressed. In this respect, many designers set out to conjoin the ordinary and society. (This attempt was not foreign to fashion designers, either.)

The goal of interior design was to restore the everyday through the designs of boutiques and restaurants. This also marked the restoration of individuality and emphasized consideration of regional and ethnic or indigenous cultures.

Industrieländern einschneidende Veränderungen brachten. Tiefgehende Diskrepanzen in der modernen Gesellschaft wurden damals offenbar. Lewis Mumford stellte fest, daß »die moderne Gesellschaft durch Energie, Massenproduktion, Standardisierung, Systematisierung, Regulierung und Vereinheitlichung gekennzeichnet ist«. Es war eine Gesellschaft, die materialistische Sättigung anstrebte und dabei von Wissenschaft und Technologie unterstützt wurde. Früher oder später mußte eine solche Gesellschaft jedoch den Glauben an die Einmaligkeit des Individuums in Frage stellen. Ein Kernproblem war, daß die Gesellschaft der Industriestaaten in ausgesprochener Angepaßtheit lebte und nicht die geringste Motivation zu einem Wandel verspürte. Der Zweck von Design im Alltagsleben ist, das Leben der Menschen zu erleichtern. Diese Funktion zielt auf die »Seele«, ein Umstand, der in letzter Zeit zunehmende Bedeutung gewinnt. Und diese Zielrichtung existierte bereits in den 60er Jahren.

Die 70er Jahre waren eine Periode des Wandels, in der man sich den Problemen zwischen Menschen, Gesellschaft und natürlicher Umwelt zuwandte. In diesem Sinne versuchten viele Designer, das Alltägliche mit der Gesellschaft in Einklang zu bringen, ein Unterfangen, das auch den Modedesignern nicht fremd war.

Ziel der Innenarchitektur war es, das Alltägliche durch die Gestaltung von Boutiquen und Restaurants wiederherzustellen. Dabei ging es auch um die Wiedereinbringung der Individualität und die Berücksichtigung regionaler und ethnischer Werte.

60. Celles-ci ont marqué une période de transformations dans les pays développés. Les conflits et les déséquilibres significatifs de la société moderne devinrent apparents. Comme l'a noté Lewis Mumford, « la société moderne se caractérise par la puissance, la production de masse, la standardisation, la systématisation, la réglementation et l'unification ». Cette société avait pour but d'arriver à une satiété matérielle, et ses efforts étaient soutenus par la science et la technologie. Cependant, cette forme de société finit par mettre au défi la croyance dans le caractère unique de l'individu. L'enjeu crucial des pays développés est que leurs sociétés sont sévèrement régulées et qu'elles ne possèdent même pas une incitation au changement. L'objectif du design dans la vie de tous les jours est d'apporter un appui à la vie des gens tels qu'ils la vivent réellement. Cette fonction met l'accent sur « l'âme », qui a récemment été soulignée dans ses nombreuses facettes. Et cet éclairage était déjà présent dans les années 60.

Les années 70 ont été une période de changement qui s'est attachée aux problèmes des rapports entre les gens, la société et l'environnement naturel. A cet égard, de nombreux designers se sont efforcés de jeter des ponts entre la vie ordinaire et la société (cette tentative a également existé dans la mode).

Le but de l'architecture intérieure a été de restaurer le quotidien à travers le design de boutiques et de restaurants. Ceci a marqué également la restauration de l'individualité, et a mis l'accent sur des considérations liées aux cultures indigènes régionales ou ethniques.

MISS ASHIDA
Boutique
Ginza, Tokyo
1992

MISS ASHIDA
Boutique
Kobe
1992

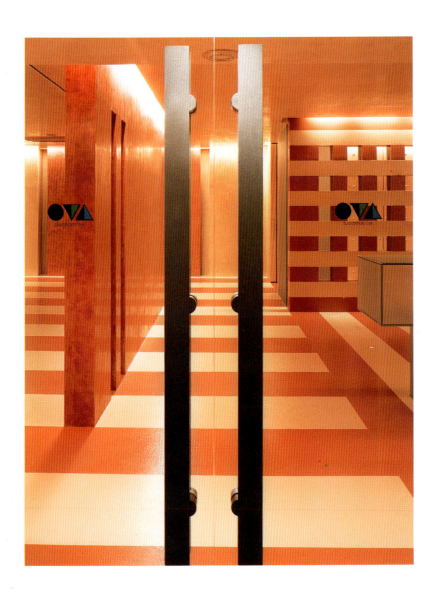

GLASSTATION OVA
Glass Showroom
Aoyama, Tokyo
1991

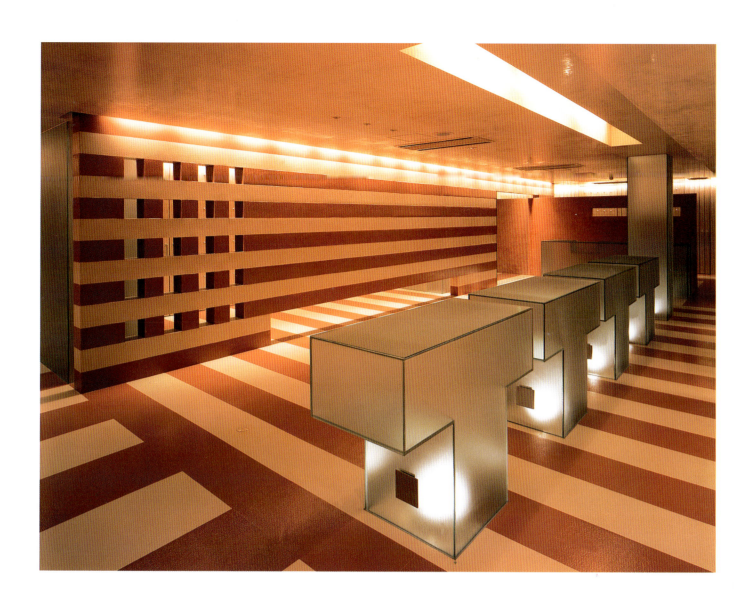

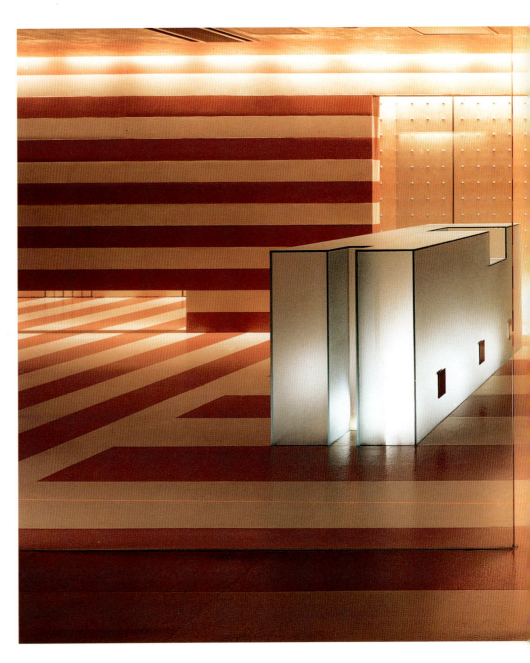

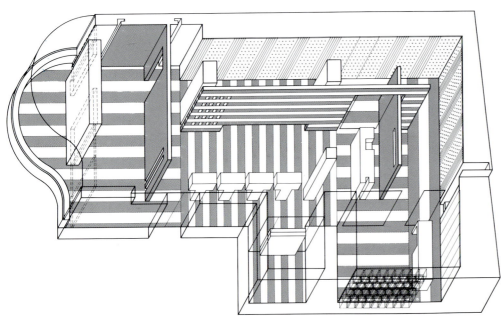

ASABA KATSUMI DESIGN STUDIO
Office
Aoyama, Tokyo
1991

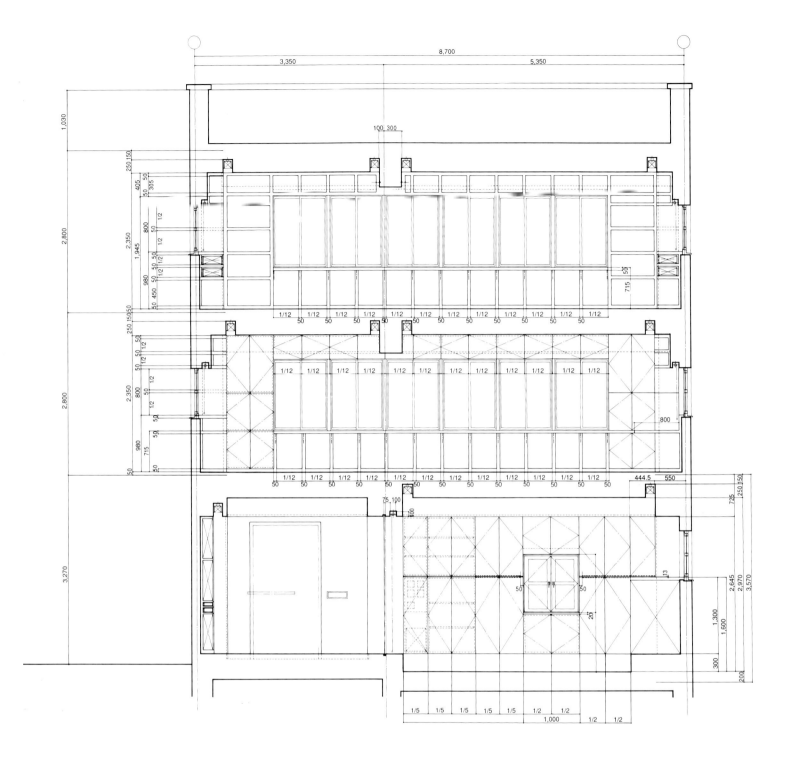

COLUMN
Shelf
1988

untitled
Chair
1988

AUGUST Chair
Chair
1989

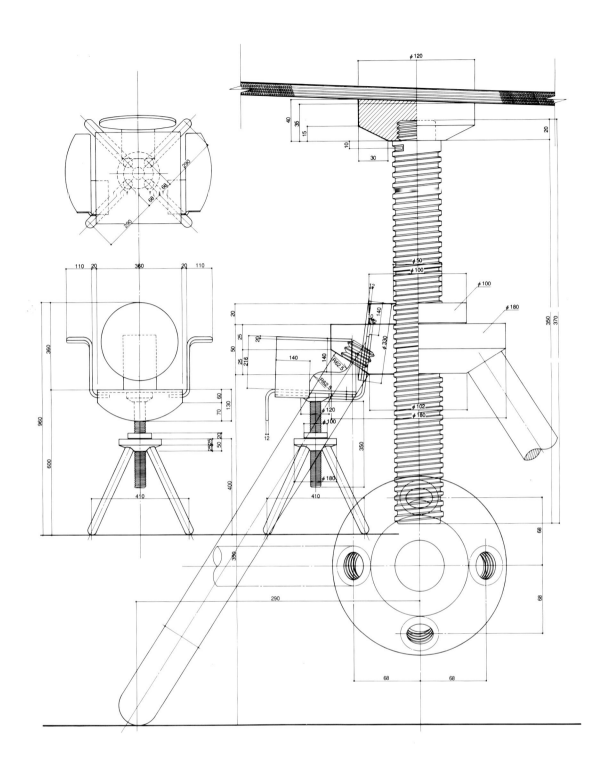

Interior Design Work
Shigeru Uchida

When appointed to conduct interior design work, I realize that an interior should not be a product of design-led work. Though it may appear that the needs of interior design created the workfield of an interior designer, the fact is that it created a loosely-knit range of work with the purpose of designing an interior.

If defined as the word indicates, interior design may be an extremely easy job: the design work inside a room. However, in reality this is a job that cannot be simply understood in a narrow sense.

Innenarchitektur
Shigeru Uchida

Wenn ich mit der Gestaltung eines Innenraums beauftragt werde, bin ich mir bewußt, daß ein Interieur nicht ausschließlich das Resultat einer Gestaltungsabsicht sein darf. Obwohl es so scheinen mag, daß die bloße Notwendigkeit von Innenarchitektur das Arbeitsfeld des Innenarchitekten bereits umrissen habe, ist dieses doch vielmehr von einer locker miteinander verbundenen Reihe von Arbeitsschritten bestimmt, deren Ziel die Gestaltung eines Innenraums ist.

Definiert man Innenarchitektur so, wie es der Begriff nahelegt, könnte es

Aménagement intérieur
Shigeru Uchida

Lorsque l'on me demande un projet d'aménagement intérieur, je suis conscient qu'un intérieur ne doit pas être simplement le produit d'un travail de design. Même si l'on peut penser que les besoins d'un tel aménagement créent le champ d'intervention de l'architecte d'intérieur, le fait est qu'ils déterminent un univers d'interventions plus ou moins liées qui ont pour objectif d'aboutir à un intérieur.

S'il est défini comme son appellation le traduit, l'aménagement intérieur peut se révéler un travail extrêmement

What we must realize is that interior design is established along with the essential meaning and content entailed in the act of returning to a space. In other words, interior design is not a creation of something that is tangible, but more an anchor-like emphasis that consolidates a chain of plans by intertwining content and the behavioural patterns required by that space. If we can accept this as true, we can also accept that final anchor-work is not the ultimate goal in interior design work. Rather, generation, conceptualization and shaping works constitute the concerns of interior design.

A design must blend and harmonize the relationship between people, society and nature. However, we find that modernization tends to sacrifice people and nature by excessively focusing on social needs.

We are now at the point, though, where we must face the need to revive a better relationship between people, society and nature.

sich um eine ausgesprochen einfache Angelegenheit handeln: die Gestaltung eines Innenraums. Tatsächlich kann diese Aufgabe nicht in einem solch engen Sinn gefaßt werden.

Wir müssen uns ins Bewußtsein rufen, daß die Aufgabe der Innenarchitektur darin besteht, einem Raum seinen wesenseigenen Bedeutungsgehalt zurückzugeben. Mit anderen Worten, Innenarchitektur bedeutet nicht, etwas Greifbares zu schaffen, vielmehr geht es darum, einen Schwerpunkt zu setzen, der eine Abfolge von Plänen vereinigt, indem er den Inhalt und die vom Raum selbst eingeforderte Verhaltensweise verknüpft. Wenn dem so ist, müssen wir eingestehen, daß die endgültige Schwerpunktsetzung nicht höchstes Ziel der Gestaltungsarbeit sein kann, sondern ihre Aufgaben in der Ideenerzeugung, Konzeptualisierung und Formgebung liegen.

Design sollte die Beziehung zwischen Individuum, Gesellschaft und Natur in Einklang bringen. Der Modernisierungsprozeß tendiert hingegen häufig dahin, das Individuum und die Natur zugunsten einer Überbewertung sozialer Anliegen zu opfern.

Wir sind jetzt an dem Punkt angelangt, wo wir uns der Notwendigkeit, das Verhältnis von Mensch, Gesellschaft und Natur zu verbessern, stellen müssen.

aisé: un travail de design sur une pièce. En réalité, ce travail ne peut être pris au seul sens étroit du terme. Nous devons réaliser que l'aménagement intérieur ne se comprend que dans son sens et son contenu essentiels induits par l'acte du retour à l'espace. En d'autres termes, l'aménagement intérieur n'est pas la création de quelque chose qui serait tangible, mais plus une accentuation, un ancrage, qui consolident une chaîne de plans en liant le contenu et les modèles de comportement requis par cet espace. Si ceci est vrai, nous pouvons accepter que le travail d'ancrage ne soit pas le but final de l'aménagement intérieur. Il s'agit plutôt de générer, de conceptualiser et de mettre en forme.

Un plan doit mêler et harmoniser les relations entre les gens, la société et la nature. Néanmoins, nous découvrons que la modernisation tend à sacrifier les gens et la nature en se concentrant excessivement sur les besoins sociaux.

Nous en sommes maintenant arrivés au point où nous devons faire face au besoin de faire revivre une meilleure relation entre l'homme, la société et la nature.

CONVERSATION
Boutique
Aoyama, Tokyo
1988

A TANTOT
Restaurant
Roppongi, Tokyo
1991

KIE
Restaurant
Azabu, Tokyo
1993

FURUKAWA RESIDENCE
Residence
Nagoya
1991

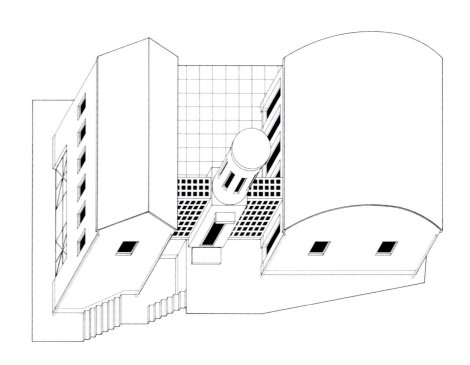

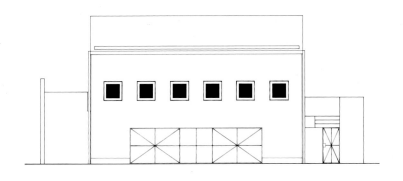

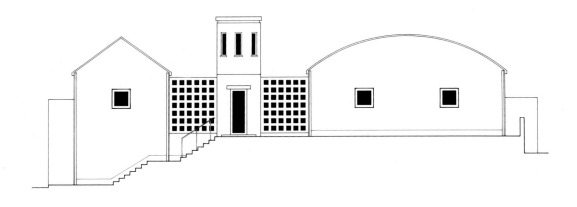

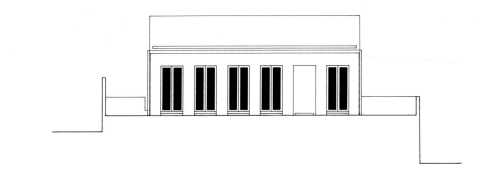

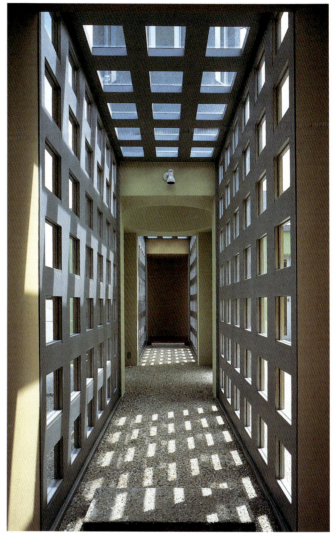

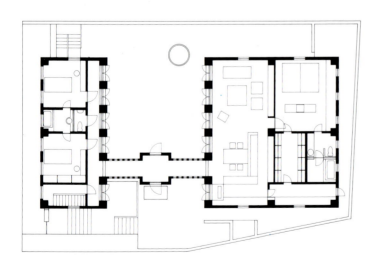

HIGURASHI RESIDENCE
Residence
Miyakejima Island, Tokyo
1988

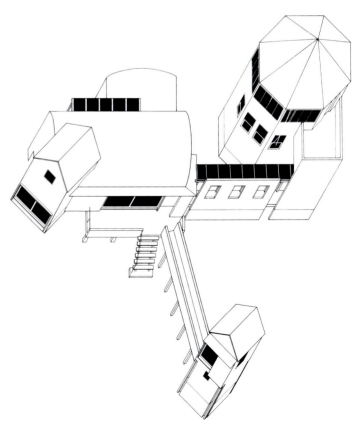

COME RAIN
Chest of Drawers
1991

COME SHINE
Chest of Drawers
1991

93

DAY BY DAY
Shelf
1991

RAMONA
Cabinet
1991

Xstage IM Series

Ikuyo Mitsuhashi

The design for the IM series started from a change in the perception of the toilet. The toilet and bathroom have been alienated from living quarters and have been frowned upon. Yet they are indispensable places for living human beings. New product design is introduced every year, but it lacks any specific logic, so it is not surprising that it heightens no one's consciousness. About the time when almost all the women's and general interest magazines in Japan began to feature articles about residential spaces, the IM series project was initiated.

Xstage IM Series

Ikuyo Mitsuhashi

Das Design der IM-Serie beruht auf einer veränderten Einstellung zur Toilette. Toilette und Badezimmer wurden von den Wohnräumen getrennt und eher stiefmütterlich behandelt. Dennoch handelt es sich um unverzichtbare Orte. Zwar werden jedes Jahr neue Produkte auf den Markt gebracht, doch in Ermangelung jeglicher inneren Logik erregen sie kaum Aufsehen. Ungefähr zu der Zeit, als fast alle japanischen Frauenzeitschriften und Illustrierten Artikel über Wohnräume zu veröffentlichen begannen, wurde die IM-Serie initiiert.

Xstage IM Series

Ikuyo Mitsuhashi

La conception de la série IM est issue d'un changement dans la perception des toilettes. Toilettes et salles de bains ont été écartées des espaces de vie normaux et regardées de haut. Ce sont néanmoins des lieux indispensables à l'être humain. De nouveaux produits sont lancés chaque année, qui manquent de toute logique spécifique, aussi n'est-il pas étonnant qu'ils n'éveillent aucun écho en nous. C'est à peu près au moment où presque tous les journaux féminins et généralistes japonais ont commencé à publier des articles sur la maison que

There is a wash-basin, where water comes out automatically if one's hands are placed under the faucet. Doctors use it in operating theatres. I was quite surprised to find this kind of basin in a public space. There was no handle anywhere when I tried to wash my hands. Someone kindly pointed out to me that there was an "instruction" notice. Every time one's hands are placed under the tap, exactly the same amount of water comes out, no matter how many times the action is repeated. Even when only a small amount of water is needed, the water runs for a certain pre-fixed length of time.

I believe that we ought to relate consciously to our tools. Especially now, when the wasteful use of natural resources is frequently discussed, it is important to maintain a sense of responsibility. Many asked me, "why two taps?" when the IM series was completed. "Because I wanted to reflect our own will more than anything else," was my reply. The idea of reflecting our own will is common throughout all the products. There are six colours and seven shapes for the tiles and the combinations are almost infinite. Of course metal fixtures and ceramics can be put together with ordinary items. I propose a bright and clean space for purposes of everyday living. But I also recognize that the products have to be individually purchased, so I can leave the actual design of the toilet and bathroom to the user.

Es gibt Waschbecken, bei denen das Wasser aus dem Hahn fließt, sobald man seine Hände darunter hält. Chirurgen beispielsweise benutzen sie in Operationssälen. Ich war daher überrascht, diese Wasserhähne an einem öffentlichen Ort vorzufinden. Als ich mir die Hände waschen wollte, gab es keinen Hahn zum Aufdrehen. Freundlicherweise verwies mich jemand auf die Bedienungsanleitung. Jedes Mal, wenn man die Hände plaziert, fließt eine exakt festgelegte Menge Wasser aus dem Hahn, ganz gleich, wie oft diese Handlung wiederholt wird. Auch wenn man eigentlich nur wenig Wasser benötigt, läuft das Wasser gemäß der vorbestimmten Zeitdauer.

Ich bin der Auffassung, daß wir mit unseren Geräten bewußter umgehen sollten. Gerade heute, wo die Verschwendung von natürlichen Ressourcen so häufig diskutiert wird, ist es wichtig, ein Gefühl der Verantwortung zu bewahren. Als die IM-Serie vorgestellt wurde, fragten mich viele Leute, warum es denn zwei Wasserhähne gebe, worauf ich erwiderte: »Weil ich vor allem erreichen wollte, daß unser eigener Wille darin zum Ausdruck kommt.« Diese Absicht liegt allen Produkten dieser Serie zugrunde. Die Kacheln gibt es in sechs Farben und sieben Formen, so daß die Kombinationen nahezu unbegrenzt sind. Natürlich können die Armaturen und Keramikteile auch mit anderen Sanitärprodukten kombiniert werden. Ich empfehle helle und klare Räume; die Einrichtungselemente sollten jedoch individuell erworben werden. Somit überlasse ich die eigentliche Gestaltung von Toilette und Bad den Benutzern.

le projet de la série IM a été initié. Il existe un lavabo dans lequel l'eau coule automatiquement dès que l'on place les mains sous le robinet. Les médecins les utilisent en salle d'opération. J'ai été surprise de trouver cette sorte de lavabo dans un lieu public. Il n'y avait pas de poignée quand j'ai essayé de me laver les mains. Quelqu'un me fit gentiment remarquer qu'il y avait un « mode d'emploi ». Chaque fois que l'on place ses mains sous le robinet, la même quantité d'eau coule, quel que soit le nombre de fois où l'action est répétée. Même si l'on n'a besoin que d'un tout petit peu d'eau, l'eau coule pendant un laps de temps fixé à l'avance.

Je pense que nous devrions avoir une relation plus consciente avec nos outils. En particulier aujourd'hui, alors que le débat sur le gaspillage des ressources naturelles est à l'ordre du jour, il est important de préserver le sens des responsabilités. Beaucoup de gens m'ont demandé lorsque la série IM fut terminée : « Pourquoi deux robinets ? » « Parce que je voulais avant tout refléter notre propre volonté », fut ma réponse. L'idée d'obéissance à notre volonté est commune à tous les autres produits de la série. On trouve six couleurs et sept formes de carrelage et les combinaisons sont presque infinies. Les accessoires en métal et les céramiques peuvent être associés à des articles ordinaires. Je propose un espace net et lumineux pour un usage quotidien. Mais je reconnais également que les produits doivent pouvoir être achetés individuellement pour laisser à l'utilisateur le design concret de ses toilettes et de sa salle de bains.

Xstage IM Series
Sanitary Ware
1987–1992

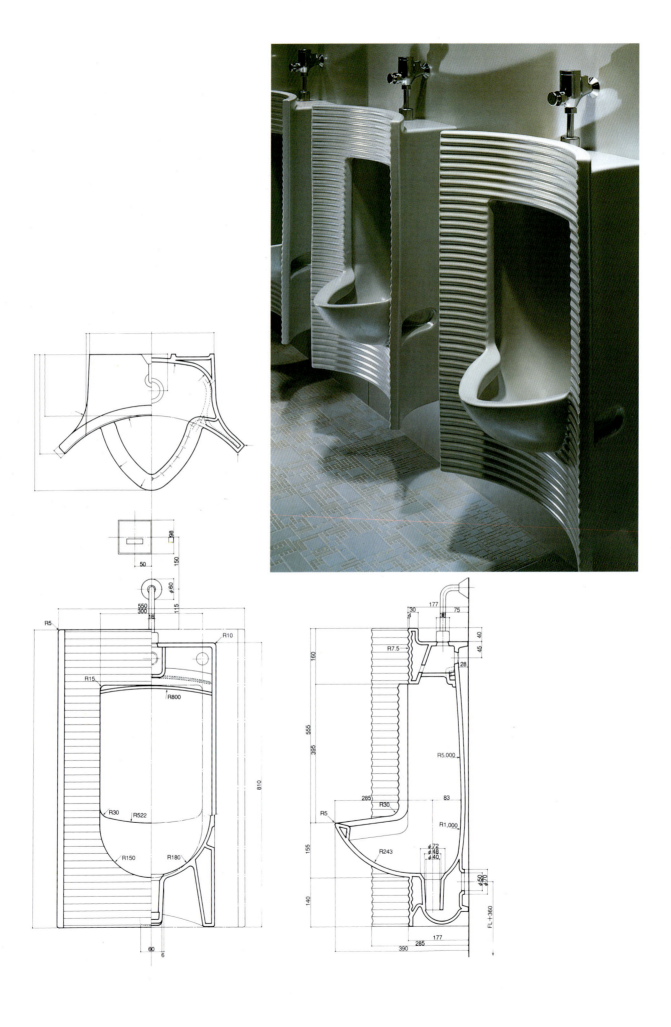

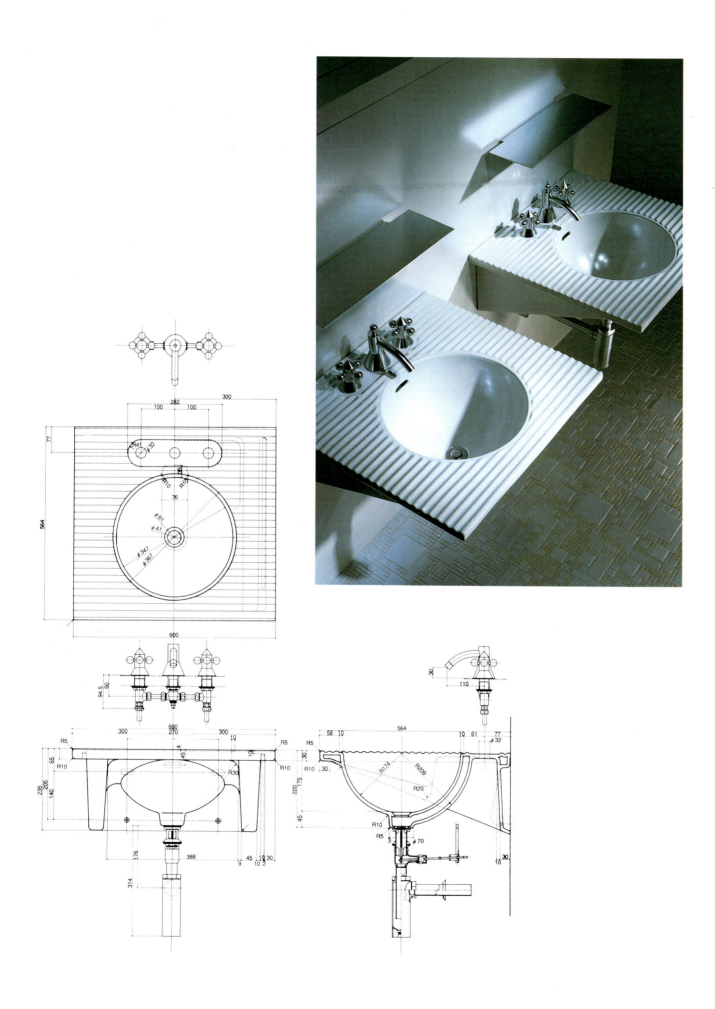

SEPTEMBER
Chair
1977

DEAR FAUSTO
Lamp
1989

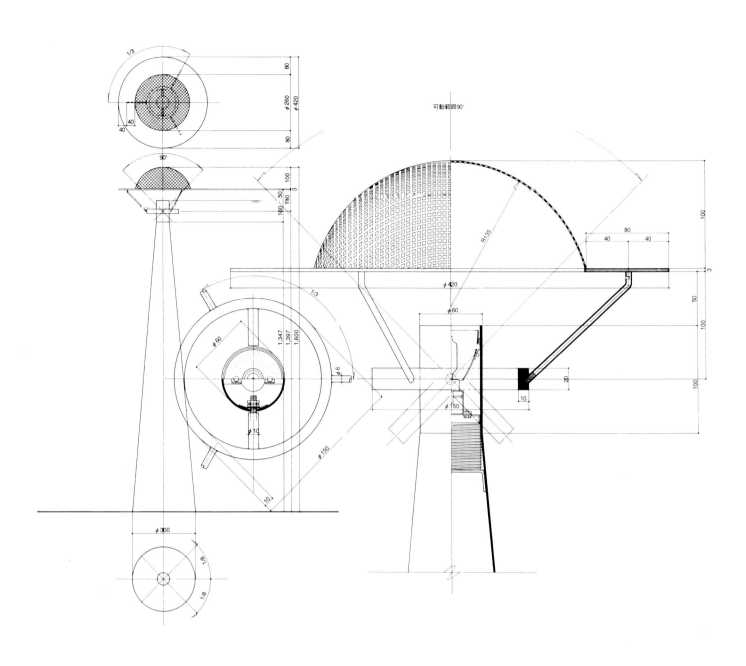

可動範囲90°

DEAR VERA
Clock
1989

DEAR MORRIS
Clock
1989

Hotel Il Palazzo

Shigeru Uchida

The plan to construct the Hotel Il Palazzo was launched in 1986 and was completed in late 1989. Before construction, the client and I started off by considering the economic and cultural concepts that we expected of this facility. This was especially necessary, since the hotel was not situated at an ideal address in Fukuoka. I do not mean to imply that it was in a dangerous location, but rather in a forgotten city that had lost its shine and glamour. Thus, there was a need to create a cultural meaning and visual attraction with the architecture

Hotel Il Palazzo

Shigeru Uchida

Der Plan für das Hotel Il Palazzo stammt aus dem Jahr 1986, fertiggestellt wurde es Ende 1989. Vor Baubeginn habe ich mit dem Auftraggeber die ökonomischen und kulturellen Ziele erörtert, die wir uns bei diesem Projekt setzten. Dies war erforderlich, da für das Hotel kein idealer Standort in Fukuoka vorgesehen war. Es handelte sich um einen vergessenen Stadtteil, dem jeglicher Glanz verloren gegangen war. Es schien also geboten, die Schaffung einer Infrastruktur für einen wenig einnehmenden Standort mit einer

Hôtel Il Palazzo

Shigeru Uchida

La construction de l'hôtel Il Palazzo a débuté en 1986 et s'est achevée fin 1989. Auparavant, le client et moi-même nous étions penchés sur les concepts à la fois économiques et culturels qui allaient sous-tendre ce projet. Cette démarche était d'autant plus utile que l'hôtel ne bénéficiait pas d'une adresse idéale à Fukuoka. Je ne veux pas dire par là qu'il s'agissait d'un site dans une zone dangereuse, mais plutôt d'une implantation dans une cité un peu oubliée qui avait perdu depuis longtemps tout brillant et tout attrait. Ainsi, devions-nous

when introducing services to such an unprepossessing site. With all this in mind, we immediately came to the conclusion that Aldo Rossi was the only miracle-worker, we could think of. The results surpassed expectations, and this single piece of architecture proved to be powerful enough to change the psychological landscape of this entire region.

My role from the start of work on the Hotel Il Palazzo was to direct the art and interior design work. The role of art director may not be familiar in a context of architectural and urban planning projects. However, modern compound architecture is only possible when many talented professionals are working through numerous confrontations. It is vital that the architecture, interior design, graphic design, lighting plan, and special interior design (in this case, a basement discotheque), as well as hotel and restaurant management, be established under a common denominator. Art direction refers to the coordinating role that adjusts the overall picture to create a uniform message. The other characteristic of the Hotel Il Palazzo is the four bars located in the annex on the left and right of the main hotel compound. This is the first attempt of its kind to create four different bars under the same theme, with the same size and shape specifications, by four different experts. We succeeded in creating four cultural fragments that consolidate the concept of the bar through the efforts of Ettore Sottsass, Shiro Kuramata, Gaetano Pesce, and Aldo Rossi.

visuell anziehenden und kulturell bedeutsamen Architektur zu verbinden. Mit diesen Vorgaben im Sinn entschieden wir uns sofort für Aldo Rossi, den einzigen »Zauberkünstler«, der uns einfiel. Das Resultat übertraf alle Erwartungen: Das Hotel verfügt über genügend Ausstrahlung, um die psychosoziale Befindlichkeit eines ganzen Viertels zu verändern.

Mir oblag von Beginn an die Leitung der künstlerischen und innenarchitektonischen Ausgestaltung des Hotels. Ein Art-Director mag im Kontext architektonischer oder stadtplanerischer Projekte ungewöhnlich erscheinen, doch ist eine moderne arbeitsteilige Architektur nur dann möglich, wenn sich viele talentierte Fachleute den zahlreichen Problemen stellen. Es ist unerläßlich, daß die Architektur und die Innenarchitektur, das Graphikdesign, die Lichtplanung und die Gestaltung spezieller Interieurs (in unserem Fall eine Discothek im Untergeschoß) ebenso wie das Hotel- und Restaurant-Management unter einen gemeinsamen Nenner gebracht werden. Dem Art-Director kommt dabei die Aufgabe der Koordination zu, die dem Gesamtbild zu einer einheitlichen Ausstrahlung verhelfen soll.

Eine weitere Besonderheit des Hotels sind die vier Bars in den Anbauten links und rechts vom Hauptgebäude. Hier wurde von vier Fachleuten erstmalig der Versuch unternommen, vier verschiedene Räume mit gleicher Bestimmung, Ausmaßen und Grundrissen zu schaffen. Das Resultat sind vier eigenwillige Interpretationen der Vorstellung »Bar«, entworfen von Ettore Sottsass, Shiro Kuramata, Gaetano Pesce und Aldo Rossi.

apporter, à travers l'architecture, un sens culturel et une séduction visuelle à ce site ingrat. Nous en sommes arrivés très vite à la conclusion que seul Aldo Rossi pouvait accomplir ce miracle. Les résultats dépassèrent nos espérances, et, à elle seule, cette œuvre architecturale allait se révéler assez forte pour modifier le paysage psychologique de toute la région.

Dès le départ, mon rôle fut de diriger les aménagement intérieurs et la partie artistique. Ce rôle de directeur artistique n'est pas très courant dans le contexte de projets architecturaux et urbanistiques. Et pourtant, l'architecture moderne composite n'est possible qu'à travers la collaboration de nombreux professionnels de talent. Il est essentiel que l'architecture, l'architecture intérieure, le design graphique, les éclairages et aménagements spéciaux (en l'occurrence, une discothèque en sous-sol), ainsi que la direction de l'hôtel et du restaurant se retrouvent sous un dénominateur commun. La direction artistique relève alors d'un rôle de coordination qui aboutit, après ajustements, à la mise au point d'un message uniforme. Les autres caractéristiques de cet hôtel sont les quatre bars situés dans l'annexe à gauche et à droite du bâtiment principal. C'était la première tentative de création de quatre lieux différents sur un même thème, avec les mêmes dimensions, les mêmes caractéristiques formelles, et réalisés par quatre créateurs différents. Nous avons réussi à créer quatre « fragments » culturels qui renforcent le concept de bar, en faisant appel à Ettore Sottsass, Shiro Kuramata, Gaetano Pesce et Aldo Rossi.

HOTEL IL PALAZZO
Hotel
Fukuoka
1989

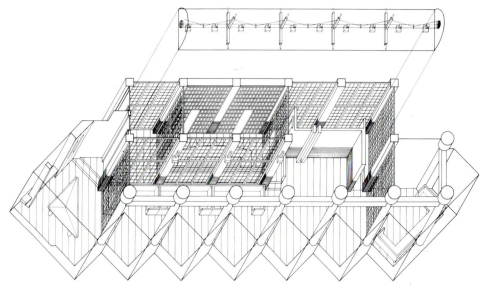

ASAHI BEER GUEST ROOM
Guest-Room
Azumabashi, Tokyo
1991

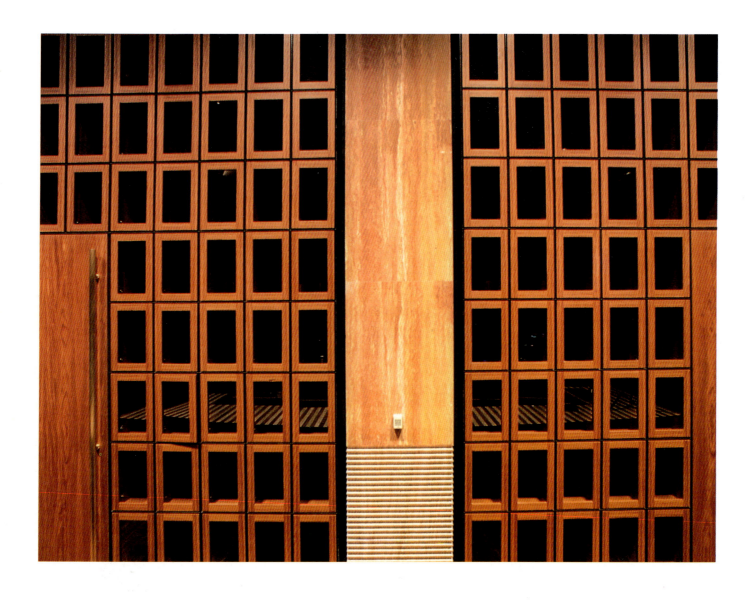

LA RANARITA
Restaurant
Azumabashi, Tokyo
1991

123

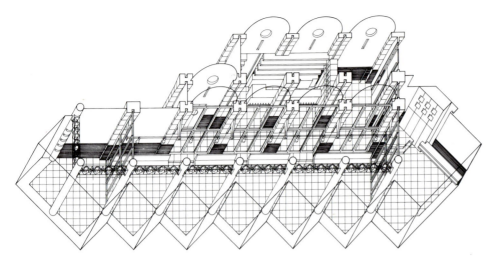

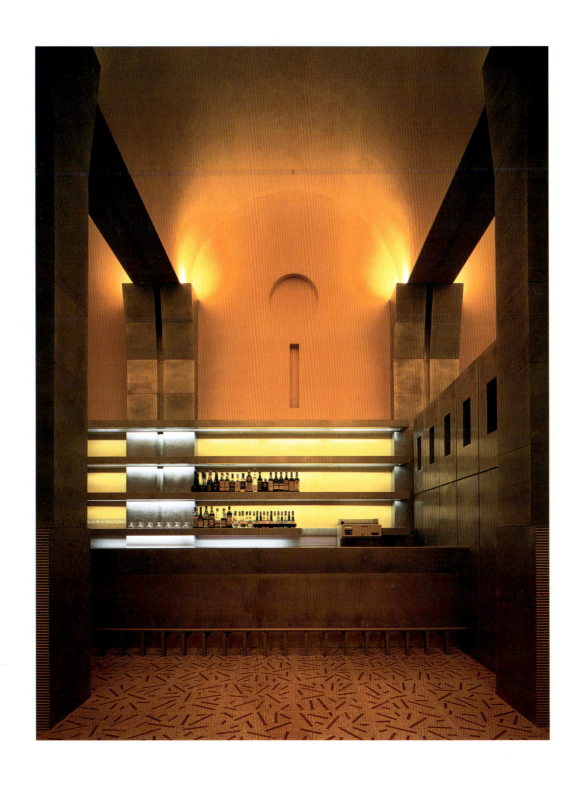

Bushoan
– Kimono Reminiscence –

Ikuyo Mitsuhashi

Until my mother's childhood, the clothing of Japan was the kimono. Saying, "I wouldn't have the occasion to wear them," and with her good grace, my mother offered me the informal kimonos she once wore as a young woman when I started to study the tea-ceremony. Thirty years and bright sunlight had made them look quite faded despite her careful attention to their storage. Murmuring, "I would have saved more of them, if I only knew you would one day be wearing them," she noticed that the formal kimonos were not there. Per-

Bushoan
– Eine Reminiszenz an den Kimono –

Ikuyo Mitsuhashi

Bis in die Kindheit meiner Mutter war das übliche Kleidungsstück in Japan der Kimono. Als ich mich mit der Teezeremonie auseinanderzusetzen begann, schenkte mir meine Mutter ihre Alltagskimonos, die sie als junge Frau getragen hatte, mit den Worten: »Ich werde ohnehin keine Gelegenheit mehr haben, sie zu tragen.« Dreißig Jahre und helles Sonnenlicht hatten dafür gesorgt, daß die Stoffe trotz sorgfältiger Aufbewahrung ausgeblichen waren. »Ich hätte auch die anderen behalten, wenn ich gewußt hätte, daß du sie eines Tages tragen

Bushoan
– Réminiscences autour d'un kimono –

Ikuyo Mitsuhashi

Lorsque ma mère était enfant, le vêtement japonais traditionnel était le kimono. Lorsque je commençai à étudier la cérémonie du thé, ma mère m'offrit avec tendresse les kimonos de tous les jours qu'elle portait jadis lorsqu'elle était jeune fille en me disant : « Je n'aurai plus l'occasion de les porter. » Trente années et l'éclat du soleil avaient fait passer leurs couleurs bien qu'ils aient été conservés avec beaucoup de soin. En murmurant : « J'aurais dû en conserver davantage, si j'avais su qu'un jour tu les porterais », elle remarqua que les

haps they had been given away for some reason. Looking at the one and a half dozen kimonos, one by one, our hearts were nearly overwhelmed by the memories rushing back from the past. Without alterations, the kimonos, would not fit me because our sizes were slightly different. To alter a kimono, it must be entirely unsewn, washed, dried and sewn back again. Unsewing a kimono evokes memories of the one who originally sewed the kimono. Unlike a machine-sewn western dress, a kimono that was made by hand, one stitch at a time, makes one sentimental when taking it apart. When I put on the kimono altered to my size, it surprisingly felt like "mine", surprisingly because it continued to bear the same old memories and it had retained its original form. "Mother's kimono" ended as the last stitch was pulled out and it became "my kimono" as it was re-sewn. Most men, hearing this kind of story, seem to feel genuinely envious. They say there is nothing of the kind left that they can inherit from their father. The kimono remains one of the few things from which we would rather not detach ourselves. If there was no opportunity for me to wear my mother's kimonos, I wonder what would have happened to them? They would have remained stored in the drawers without seeing the light of day, so long as my mother chose not to wear them. Working on the Bushoan project reminded me of many forgotten but important things. We clearly see what is in front of us, but we must also not forget to look back from time to time.

würdest«, murmelte sie, als sie feststellte, daß ihre festlichen Kimonos nicht mehr da waren. Als wir jeden einzelnen der 18 Kimonos betrachteten, wurden wir von den dabei wachgerufenen Erinnerungen überwältigt. Da wir unterschiedliche Konfektionsgrößen hatten, paßten mir die Kimonos ohne Änderungen nicht. Sämtliche Nähte mußten gelöst und schließlich neu vernäht werden. Das Auftrennen eines Kimonos läßt uns an die Person denken, die ihn ursprünglich Stich für Stich genäht hat, was bei einem maschinell produzierten westlichen Kleidungsstück nicht vorstellbar wäre. Als ich den auf meine Größe geänderten Kimono überstreifte, fühlte er sich überraschend an wie »meiner«, überraschend, denn nach wie vor löste er Erinnerungen aus und hatte ja auch seine ursprüngliche Form behalten. Beim Lösen der letzten Naht hatte »Mutters Kimono« aufgehört zu existieren, durch das Zusammennähen ist er dann zu »meinem« geworden. Die meisten Männer scheinen, wenn sie eine solche Geschichte hören, neidisch zu werden, da sie glauben, daß ihre Väter ihnen nichts Vergleichbares vererben könnten. Ein Kimono gehört zu den wenigen Dingen, von denen wir uns nur ungern trennen. Ich frage mich, was mit den Kimonos meiner Mutter geschehen wäre, wenn ich nicht die Gelegenheit gehabt hätte, sie zu tragen. Sie wären wahrscheinlich in ihren Schubladen verblieben. Die Arbeit an dem Bushoan-Projekt erinnerte mich an viele vergessene, aber wichtige Dinge. Wir beschäftigen uns zwar intensiv mit der Zukunft, doch müssen wir von Zeit zu Zeit auch unseren Blick in die Vergangenheit richten.

kimonos de cérémonie manquaient. Peut-être avaient-ils déjà été donnés ? En détaillant ces 18 kimonos, un par un, nos cœurs s'emplirent de souvenirs surgis du passé. Sans retouche, ils ne pouvaient m'aller car nos tailles étaient légèrement différentes. Pour retoucher un kimono, il doit être entièrement décousu, lavé, séché et recousu. Découdre un kimono fait revivre les souvenirs de celui qui l'a cousu à l'origine. A la différence des vêtements occidentaux faits à la machine, un kimono se coud à la main, point par point, et l'émotion vous étreint lorsque vous le démontez. Lorsque je revêtis un kimono remis à ma taille, je sentis immédiatement, à ma grande surprise, qu'il était devenu « mien », même s'il continuait à évoquer les mêmes anciens souvenirs conservés de son apparence antérieure. Le « kimono de ma mère » finit son existence avec le dernier fil tiré, et devint « mon kimono » en étant recousu. La plupart des hommes, qui entendent ce genre d'histoire, manifestent leur envie. Ils disent que leur père ne peut rien leur léguer de ce genre. Le kimono reste l'une des rares choses dont nous voudrions ne jamais nous détacher. Si je n'avais pas l'opportunité de porter les kimonos de ma mère, je me demande ce qui leur serait arrivé ? Tant que ma mère aurait décidé de ne plus les porter, ils seraient restés rangés dans des tiroirs sans plus jamais voir la lumière du jour. Travailler sur le projet Bushoan m'a rappelé de nombreuses choses oubliées, mais importantes. Nous voyons clairement ce qui est devant nos yeux, mais nous ne devons pas oublier de regarder de temps en temps en arrière.

BUSHOAN An Achievement of a Decade
Exhibition
Aoyama, Tokyo
1987

ORIJINZA
Exhibition
Aoyama, Tokyo
1991

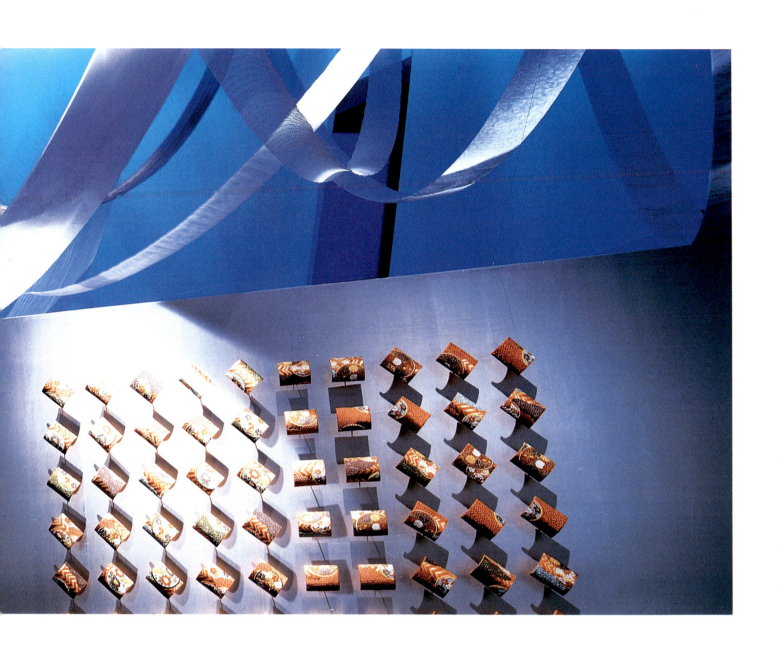

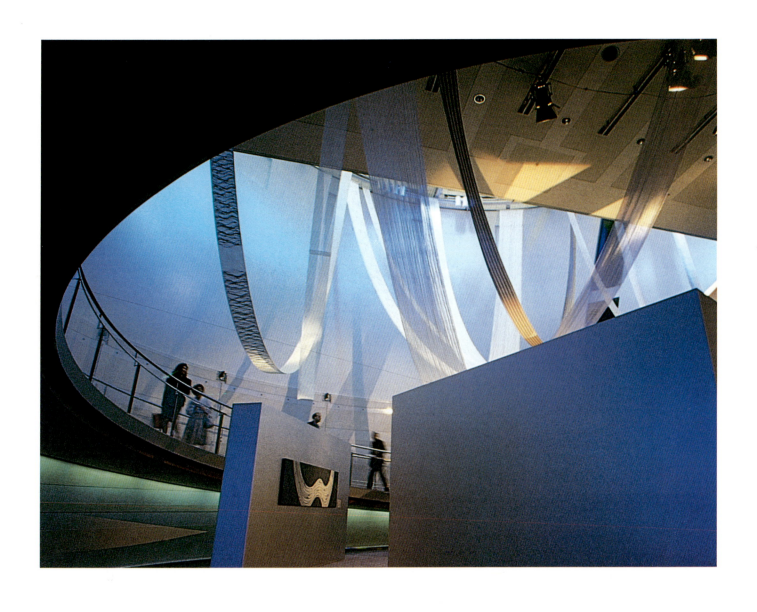

KIMIKO BY KIMIKO
Exhibition
Aoyama, Tokyo
1990

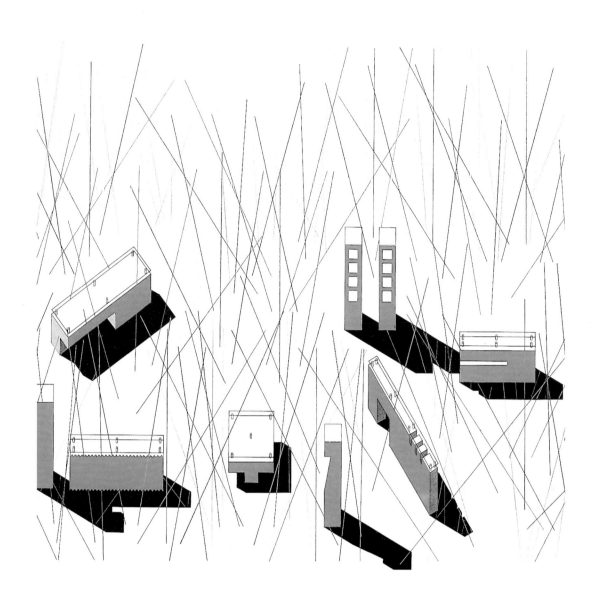

untitled
Table
1992

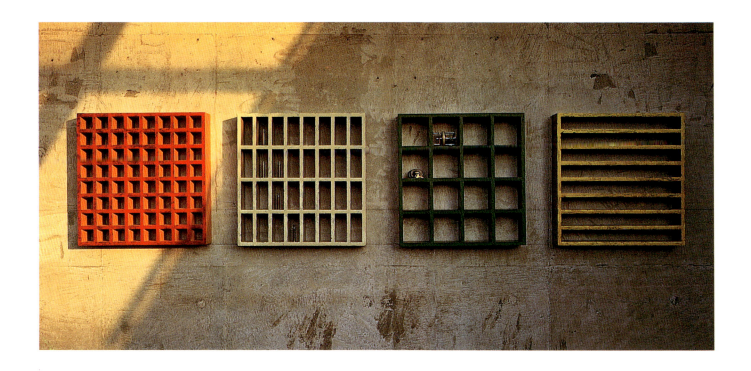

untitled
Shelf
1995

MIRAI-CHASHITSU
Office
Hakozaki, Fukuoka
1990

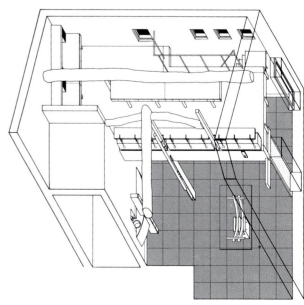

Shikimi (Threshold)
Shigeru Uchida

The *nijo-daime* (two-tatami mat tearooms) were prepared for a fair sponsored by a porcelain manufacturer under the theme, *shikimi*.

In Japan, there is a unique term, *shikimi*. This expression indicates a threshold that separates the inside from the outside of a gate. It also serves as a doorsill below a door, *shoji* (sliding) screen, or *fusuma* (sliding) door. A term not currently used in daily conversation, it originally had psychological connotations. There is a colloquialism that goes, "the threshold is too high to cross over". This

Shikimi (Schwelle)
Shigeru Uchida

Die *nijo-daime* (Teeräume von der Größe zweier Tatamimatten) wurden für eine von einem Porzellanhersteller gesponserten Messe eingerichtet, die unter dem Thema *shikimi* stand.

Der japanische Begriff *shikimi* bezeichnet die Schwelle, die bei einem Durchgang das Innere von dem Äußeren trennt. Gleichzeitig bezeichnet er aber auch die hölzernen Führungsschienen traditioneller japanischer Schiebetüren, der *fusuma* (Schiebetüren, die das Haus nach außen öffnen) und der *shoji* (Schiebetüren im Inneren eines Hauses).

Shikimi (Le seuil)
Shigeru Uchida

Ces *nijo-daime* (salles de thé à deux tatami) ont été conçues pour une foire financée par un fabricant de porcelaine sur le thème du *shikimi*.

Au Japon, le terme de *shikimi* est unique. Il exprime une ligne qui sépare l'intérieur de l'extérieur. Il signifie également le seuil sous une porte, un écran *shoji* (coulissant) ou une porte *fusuma* (coulissante). Néanmoins nous ne l'utilisons pas dans la conversation courante ; à l'origine, il avait une signification psychologique. L'expression courante, « le seuil est trop haut pour être franchi », ne se

does not refer to the difficulty of passing over a threshold because of the height or shape of it, but rather to the psychological barrier that prevents one from crossing the threshold to enter the house. There are a lot of factors which affect our consciousness of a threshold in our architecture and customs.

The *sekimori* stone is an example of this psychological effect. The symbolic emphasis of placing a stone wrapped with rope in front of a garden implies a message to warn an outsider against proceeding any further.

A *torii* gate erected at the entrance of a shrine plays the same role. It is a *kekkai* (boundary) that differentiates the sacred (inside gate) from the profane (outside gate). We call these psychological regulators of space a *shiki-iki* (limen). The *shikiiki* and *shikimi* are interchangeable, since *shikiiki* indicates a generation or loss of a psychological *kekkai*, that is a boundary that conveys a psychological message.

The *sukiya* (typical Japanese architecture) or tea-rooms also manifest this psychological response. The three *nijo-daime* that you see here aim to

create such awareness through particularly small spaces.

Der Begriff wird in der heutigen Alltagssprache nicht verwendet, er faßt ursprünglich psychologische Konnotationen. Die Redewendung »diese Schwelle ist zu hoch für mich« meint nicht die physische Schwierigkeit beim Überqueren einer Türschwelle aufgrund ihrer Höhe oder Form. Vielmehr wird auf eine psychologische Schranke verwiesen, die einen vom Übertreten der Schwelle abhält. Eine Vielzahl wird von Faktoren bestimmt unsere Wahrnehmung von Schranken in der Architektur oder im Rahmen von Sitten und Bräuchen.

Als Beispiel für einen solchen psychologischen Effekt kann der *sekimori*-Stein gelten: Symbolisch impliziert der von einem Seil umwickelte Stein am Eingang des Gartens eine Warnung, die einen Fremden vom Eintreten abhalten soll. Die gleiche Funktion hat das *torii*-Portal, das vor einem Schrein aufgestellt ist. Es markiert ein *kekkai* (Grenze), das das Heilige (inneres Tor) vom Profanen (äußeres Tor) trennt. Wir bezeichnen diese psychologischen Regulative von Raum als *shikiiki* (Schranken). *Shikiiki* und *shikimi* sind gleichbedeutend, da *shikiiki*

auf die Errichtung oder den Fall eines *kekkai* hinweist, also einer psychologisch implizierten Grenze.

Das *sukiya* (traditionelle japanische Architektur) und damit auch die Teeräume manifestieren dieses psychologische Beziehungsgeflecht. Die drei hier vorgestellten *nijo-daime* wollen diesen Effekt durch betont kleine Räume erzeugen.

réfère pas à la difficulté de franchir la hauteur ou la forme d'un seuil, mais plutôt à l'effet psychologique qui empêche quelqu'un de franchir celui d'une maison. Un grand nombre de facteurs affectent notre conscience de ce seuil, dans notre architecture comme dans nos coutumes.

La pierre *sekimori* est un exemple de cet effet psychologique. La marque symbolique – placer une pierre entourée de corde devant un jardin – implique l'avertissement donné à un intrus de ne pas aller plus loin. Une porte *torii* érigée à l'entrée d'un sanc-

tuaire joue le même rôle. C'est un *kekkai* (limite) qui fait frontière entre le sacré (côté intérieur de la porte) et le profane (à l'extérieur). Nous appelons ces éléments régulateurs d'espace un *shikiiki* (limite). Le *shikiiki* et le *shikimi* sont interchangeables, puisque *shikiiki* indique la naissance ou la perte d'un *kekkai* psychologique, qui est une frontière véhiculant un message psychologique.

Le *sukiya* (typique de l'architecture japonaise) ou salle de thé manifeste également cet effet psychologique. Les trois *nijo-daime* que vous voyez ici

veulent créer une conscience de ce type dans des espaces extrêmement réduits.

NIJO-DAIME SHIN
Tea-Room
1989

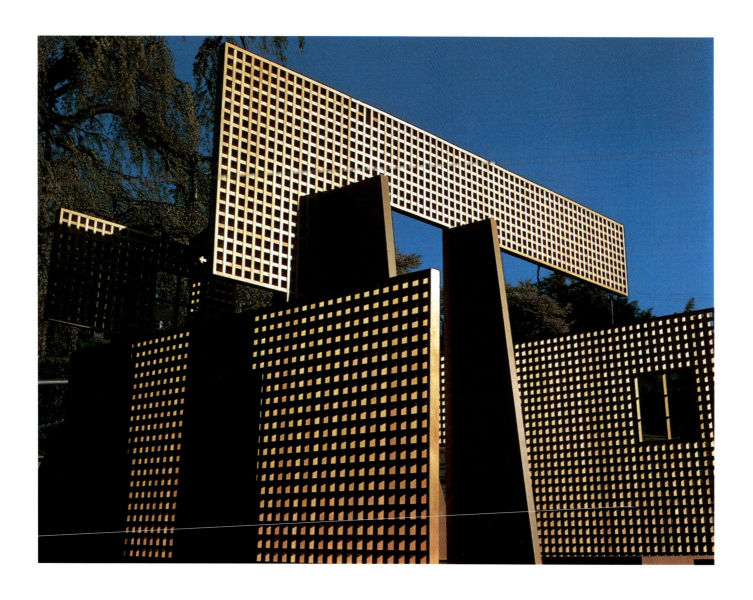

NIJO-DAIME SO
Tea-Room
1989

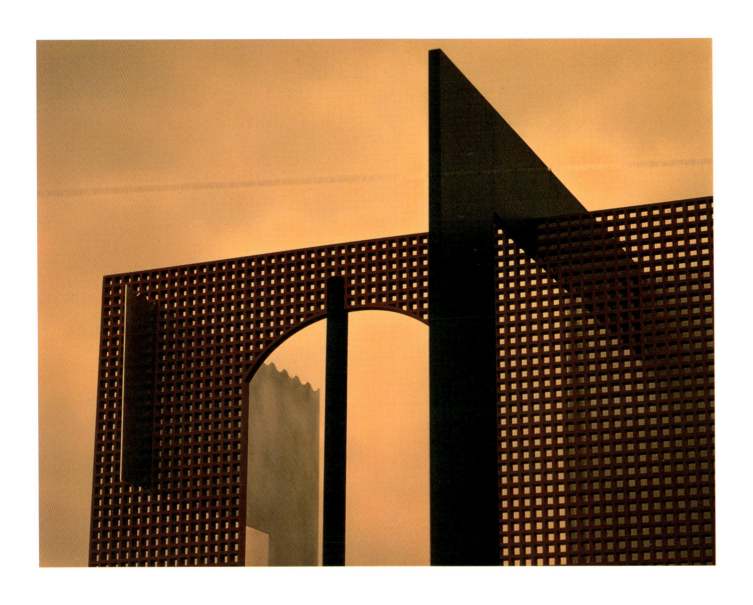

FREE FORM CHAIR
Chair
1969

NIBANKAN
Bar
Shinjuku, Tokyo
1970

CAFE DEUX
Restaurant
Ichikawa
1970

SAKATA DENTAL CLINIC
Dental Clinic
Sapporo
1971

ALICANTE
Restaurant
Shibuya, Tokyo
1971

BALCON
Bar
Roppongi, Tokyo
1973

1969–

BLACK FURNITURE
Cabinet
1973

RATTAN CHAIR
Chair
1974

SHIKIMI Exhibition
Exhibition
Aoyama, Tokyo
1974

U-ATELIER
Villa
Yamanakako
1974

WEEKEND HOUSE
Villa
Yamanakako
1974

GROUP PAM
Office
Meguro, Tokyo
1976

V-HOUSE
Villa
Yamanakako
1976

YOSHINOTO
Apparel Showroom
Nihonbashi, Tokyo
1977

ABBY
Bar
Roppongi, Tokyo
1977

HAI
Boutique
Shibuya, Tokyo
1977

OCTOBER
Chair
1977

SEPTEMBER
Chair
1977
The Metropolitan Museum of Art, New York

1976–

RESIDENCE IN ASAGAYA
Residence
Asagaya, Tokyo
1977

PRONTO
Bar
Azabu, Tokyo
1978

ISSEY MIYAKE
Boutique
Chiba
1978

A-STUDIO
Office
Harajuku, Tokyo
1978

OZUSHI
Restaurant
Azabu, Tokyo
1978

JARRETT
Bar
Fukuoka
1979
Tile Design: Tadanori Yokoo

RESIDENCE IN HAKOZAKI
Residence
Fukuoka
1979

MATSUKI
Bar
Shibuya, Tokyo
1980

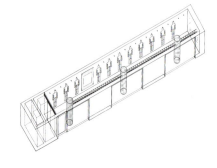

ISSEY SPORTS
Boutique
Takamatsu
1980

ISSEY SPORTS SAND PIPER
Boutique
Osaka
1981

NIRVANA
Chair
1981
Montreal Museum of Decorative Arts

PRESENTATION FOR THREE SHOPS
Exhibition
Ginza, Tokyo
1981

1979–

A TANTOT
Restaurant
Roppongi, Tokyo
1981
Marble Patterns: Ikko Tanaka

KISSA
Shoe Store
Shibuya, Tokyo
1981

HONBO REAL ESTATE
Office
Aoyama, Tokyo
1982

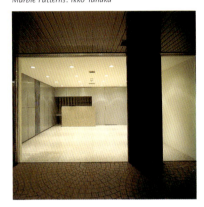

IGARASHI SHOWROOM
Showroom
Aoyama, Tokyo
1982

YOHJI YAMAMOTO
Boutique
Ikebukuro, Tokyo
1983

KURIGAMI STUDIO
Photographer's Studio
Kaigan, Tokyo
1983

KISSA
Shoe Store
Kobe
1983

A-ATELIER
Villa
Yamanakako
1983

CABARET VOLTAIRE
Bar
Sapporo
1984

49AV JUNKO SHIMADA
Boutique
Shibuya, Tokyo
1984

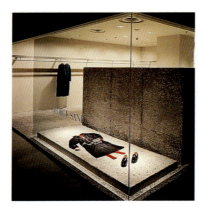

GEORGE SAND
Boutique
Shibuya, Tokyo
1984

Y'S FOR MEN
YOHJI YAMAMOTO POUR HOMME
Boutique
Kyoto
1984

1983–

Y'S SUPERPOSITION
Boutique
Aoyama, Tokyo
1984

Y'S
Boutique
Shibuya, Tokyo
1984

BUSHOAN Exhibition
Exhibition
Akasaka, Tokyo
1984

POSH HYOJITO BUILDING
Office
Aoyama, Tokyo
1984

KOSHINO RESIDENCE
Residence
Aoyama, Tokyo
1984

ROMANISCHES CAFE
Bar
Roppongi, Tokyo
1985
Drawings on Tiles: Seitaro Kuroda

LE CLUB
Bar
Azabu, Tokyo
1985

GEORGE SAND
Boutique
Aoyama, Tokyo
1985

SUIVI. Exhibition
Exhibition
Akasaka, Tokyo
1985

COPPELIA
Modern Ballet Stage
Gotanda, Tokyo
1985

HIGURASHI RESIDENCE
Residence
Aoyama, Tokyo
1985

YUZUTEI
Restaurant
Azabu, Tokyo
1985

1985–

IMAI
Restaurant
Azabu, Tokyo
1985

LE CLUB
Bar
Roppongi, Tokyo
1986

MPATA
Boutique
Shibuya, Tokyo
1986

CLERMONT
Boutique
Ashiya
1986

HANAE MORI TISSUE
Boutique
Aoyama, Tokyo
1986

RENAISSANCE
Boutique
Kyoto
1986

YOHJI YAMAMOTO
YOHJI YAMAMOTO POUR HOMME
Boutique
Kobe
1986

SEISEIAN
Boutique
Ginza, Tokyo
1986

SUIVI.
Boutique
Ginza, Tokyo
1986

NY CHAIR II
Chair
1986
San Francisco Museum of Modern Art

WEISER RESIDENCE
Residence
New York
1986
Collaborator: Toshiko Mori

TIZIO
Restaurant
Fukuoka
1986

1986–

IMAI
Restaurant
Osaka
1986

SASAN
Restaurant
Daikanyama, Tokyo
1986

NY WALL UNIT
Shelf
1986

NY SIDEBOARD
Sideboard
1986

Concept Model-LE CLUB
Bar
Kobe
1987

Concept Model-Y'S FOR MEN
Boutique
Kyoto
1987

COSA-NOSTRA
Boutique
Kobe
1987

TAKEDA SACHIYO
Boutique
Hiroo, Tokyo
1987

ESPRIT KIDS
Boutique
Washington D.C.
1987

ESPRIT SHELF COMPONENT SYSTEM
Boutique, Shelf Component System
1987

BUSHOAN *An Achievement of a Decade*
Exhibiton
Aoyama, Tokyo
1987

CONVERSATION
Boutique
Aoyama, Tokyo
1988
Logo Design: Shin Matsunaga
Lighting Design: Harumi Fujimoto

1987–

DANIEL HECHTER
Boutique
Pusan
1988

untitled
Chair
1988

CONVERSATION *Exhibition*
Exhibition
Aoyama, Tokyo
1988

YATAI MOVABLE ARCHITECTURE
Exhibition
Nagoya
1988

ITCHOH
Restaurant
Aoyama, Tokyo
1988
Logo Design: Koichi Sato

COLUMN
Shelf
1988

HIGURASHI RESIDENCE
Villa
Miyakejima Island, Tokyo
1988

AUGUST Chair
Chair
1989
Manufacturer: MATERA

DEAR MORRIS
Clock
1989
Manufacturer: ACERBIS INTERNATIONAL
Montreal Museum of Decorative Arts

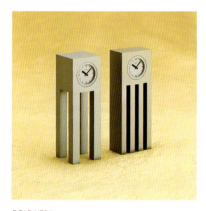

DEAR VERA
Clock
1989
Manufacturer: ALESSI
Montreal Museum of Decorative Arts

HOTEL IL PALAZZO
Hotel
Fukuoka
1989
Architect: Aldo Rossi/Morris Adjmi, SDA U.S.A.
Associate Architect: Mitsuru Kaneko, Dan Sekkei
Architectural Coordination: Toyota Horiguchi,
SDA Japan
Lighting Design: Harumi Fujimoto
General Graphic Design: Ikko Tanaka
Copy Writing: Shinzo Higurashi

AOYAMA-MIHONCHO
Paper Showroom
Shibuya, Tokyo
1989
Logo Design: Shin Matsunaga
Naming: Shinzo Higurashi

1988−

DEAR FAUSTO
Lamp
1989

NIJO-DAIME SHIN
Tea-Room
1989

NIJO-DAIME SO
Tea-Room
1989

MICALADY
Boutique
Ginza, Tokyo
1990

KITAJIMA
Confectionery
Saga
1990

KIMIKO BY KIMIKO
Exhibition
Aoyama, Tokyo
1990
Lighting Design: Harumi Fujimoto

MIRAI-CHASHITSU
Office
Fukuoka
1990

CHERRY WOOD I
Cabinet
1991

CHERRY WOOD II
Cabinet
1991

STORMY WEATHER
Shelf
1991

RAMONA
Cabinet
1991
Manufacturer: UMS PASTOE B.V.

COME RAIN
Chest of Drawers
1991
Manufacturer: UMS PASTOE B.V.

1990–

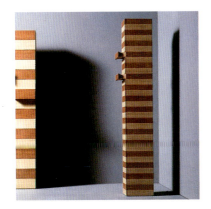

COME SHINE
Chest of Drawers
1991
Manufacturer: UMS PASTOE B.V.

ORIJINZA
Exhibition
Aoyama, Tokyo
1991
Lighting Design: Harumi Fujimoto

GLASSTATION OVA
Glass Showroom
Aoyama, Tokyo
1991

ASAHI BEER GUEST ROOM
Guest-Room
Azumabashi, Tokyo
1991
Lighting Design: Harumi Fujimoto

ASABA KATSUMI DESIGN STUDIO
Office
Aoyama, Tokyo
1991
Architect: Aldo Rossi

FURUKAWA RESIDENCE
Residence
Nagoya
1991

A TANTOT
Restaurant
Roppongi, Tokyo
1991
Wall Painting: Masuteru Aoba

LA RANARITA
Restaurant
Azumabashi, Tokyo
1991
Lighting Design: Harumi Fujimoto

DAY BY DAY
Shelf
1991
Manufacturer: UMS PASTOE B.V.

MIND GEAR
Altar Box
1992

MISS ASHIDA
Boutique
Ginza, Tokyo
1992

MISS ASHIDA
Boutique
Kobe
1992

1991 –

HORIZONTAL
Cabinet
1992

VERTICAL Series
Cabinet
1992

TOBU DEPARTMENT STORE
Department Store
Ikebukuro, Tokyo
1992

HAKKAKU-FUKAGATA URUSHIBACHI
Octagonal Bowl
1992
Manufacturer: PRODUCT-U

EAST OF THE SUN
Table
1992

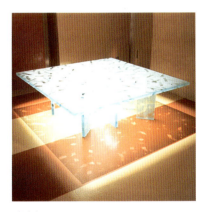

untitled
Table
1992

Xstage IM Series
Sanitary Ware
1987–1992

JUN ASHIDA
Boutique
Daikanyama, Tokyo
1993

KIE
Restaurant
Azabu, Tokyo
1993

JI-AN, GYO-AN, SO-AN
Tea-Room
1993

MIZUSASHI
Fresh Water Container
1994

ROKKAKU-SUEHIRO MIZUSASHI
Hexagonal Cone Vase
1994

1992–

ROKKAKU-SUEHIRO GAMA
Hexagonal Kettle
1994

SHIMAZU MEDICAL CLINIC
Medical Clinic
Shimokitazawa, Tokyo
1994

HI, TSUKI, MOKU, KA, DO, GON, SUI
Tea-Scoop
1994

KYOTO HOTEL (LOBBY)
Hotel
Kyoto
1994

OSAKA WORLD TRADE CENTER
(BAY ROOST)
Bar
Osaka
1995

DR. BAELTZ
Shop
Shimokitazawa, Tokyo
1995

Shigeru Uchida, Ikuyo Mitsuhashi, Toru Nishioka

Shigeru Uchida

1943	Born in Yokohama
1966	Graduated from Kuwasawa Design School in Tokyo
1970	Established Uchida Design Studio
1973–	Lecturer at Kuwasawa Design School
1974–78	Lecturer at Tokyo University of Art & Design
1981	Established Studio 80
	Received the Japan Interior Designer's Association Award
1987	Received the Mainichi Design Award
1988	Permanent Collection: *September* armchair/The Metropolitan Museum of Art, New York
1990	Received the Best Store of the Year Special Award and the Shokankyo Design Award '90 Grand Prize
1992	Permanent Collection: *NY Chair II* armchair, *Tenderly* floor lamp,/San Francisco Museum of Modern Art
1993	Permanent Collection: *Nirvana* chair, *Dear Morris* clock/Montreal Museum of Decorative Arts
	Received the First Kuwasawa Design Award

PUBLICATIONS

Studio 80/1985/G. PAM
Residential Interiors/1986/Shinchosha
Interiors of Uchida, Mitsuhashi & Studio 80/1987/Rikuyosha Publishing Inc.
The Era of Chairs/1988/Kobunsha Publishing
Hotel IL PALAZZO – A City Stimulated by Architecture – /1990/Rikuyosha Publishing Inc. (co-author)
Architecture Riffle Series Hotel IL PALAZZO/1992/TOTO Publishing
Architecture Riffle Series Three Nijo-Daime/1993/TOTO Publishing
JAPAN INTERIOR vol.1–4/1994/Rikuyosha Publishing Inc. (co-author/Kenji Oki)

1943	Geboren in Yokohama
1966	Studienabschluß an der Kuwasawa Design School in Tokio
1970	Gründet das Uchida Design Studio
1973–	Lehrauftrag an der Kuwasawa Design School
1974–78	Lehrauftrag an der University of Art & Design in Tokio
1981	Gründet das Studio 80
	Auszeichnung mit dem Japan Interior Designer's Association Award
1987	Auszeichnung mit dem Mainichi Design Award
1988	Aufnahme des Sessels *September* in die Sammlung des New Yorker Metropolitan Museum of Art
1990	Auszeichnung mit dem Best Store of the Year Special Award sowie dem Shokankyo Design Award '90 Grand Prize
1992	Aufnahme des Sessels *NY Chair II* und der Standleuchte *Tenderly* in die Sammlung des San Francisco Museum of Modern Art
1993	Aufnahme des Stuhls *Nirvana* und der Uhr *Dear Morris* in die Sammlung des Montreal Museum of Decorative Arts; Auszeichnung mit dem First Kuwasawa Design Award

PUBLIKATIONEN

Studio 80/1985/G. PAM
Residential Interiors/1986/Shinchosha
Interiors of Uchida, Mitsuhashi & Studio 80/1987/Rikuyosha Publishing Inc.
The Era of Chairs/1988/Kobunsha Publishing
Hotel II PALAZZO – A City Stimulated by Architecture – /1990/Rikuyosha Publishing Inc. (Co-Autor)
Architecture Riffle Series Hotel II PALAZZO/1992/TOTO Publishing
Architecture Riffle Series Three Nijo-Daime/1993/TOTO Publishing
JAPAN INTERIOR Bd. 1–4/1994/Rikuyosha Publishing Inc. (Co-Autor/Kenji Oki)

1943	Naissance à Yokohama
1966	Diplôme de la Kuwasawa Design School de Tokyo
1970	Crée le Uchida Design Studio
1973–	Conférencier à la Kuwasawa Design School
1974–78	Conférencier à la Tokyo University of Art & Design
1981	Crée le Studio 80
	Obtient le Japan Interior Designer's Association Award
1987	Obtient le Mainichi Design Award
1988	Son fauteuil *September* figure dans la collection permanente du Metropolitan Museum of Art, New York
1990	Obtient le Best Store of the Year Special Award et le Shokankyo Design Award '90 Grand Prize
1992	Son fauteuil *NY Chair II* et son lampadaire *Tenderly* figurent dans la collection permanente du San Francisco Museum of Modern Art
1993	Son fauteuil *Nirvana* et son horloge *Dear Morris* figurent dans la collection permanente du Montreal Museum of Decorative Arts
	Obtient le First Kuwasawa Design Award

PUBLICATIONS

Studio 80/1985/G. PAM
Residential Interiors/1986/Shinchosha
Interiors of Uchida, Mitsuhashi & Studio 80/1987/Rikuyosha Publishing Inc.
The Era of Chairs/1988/Kobunsha Publishing
Hotel IL PALAZZO – A City Stimulated by Architecture – /1990/Rikuyosha Publishing Inc. (coauteur)
Architecture Riffle Series Hotel IL PALAZZO/1992/TOTO Publishing
Architecture Riffle Series Three Nijo-Daime/1993/TOTO Publishing
JAPAN INTERIOR vol.1–4/1994/Rikuyosha Publishing Inc. (coauteur/Kenji Oki)

Ikuyo Mitsuhashi

1944	Born in Tokyo
1966	Graduated from Tama Art University in Tokyo
1970	Joined Uchida Design Studio
1977	Established Ikuyo Mitsuhashi Atelier
1984	Joined Studio 80
1987	Received the Glass Design Grand Prize of the NSG Shop & Display Contest
1991 –	Lecturer at Musashino Art University

PUBLICATIONS
Studio 80/1985/G. PAM
Interiors of Uchida, Mitsuhashi & Studio 80/1987/
Rikuyosha Publishing Inc.
Hotel IL PALAZZO – A City Stimulated by
Architecture – /1990/Rikuyosha Publishing Inc.
(co-author)

1944	Geboren in Tokio
1966	Studienabschluß an der Tama Art University in Tokio
1970	Eintritt in das Uchida Design Studio
1977	Gründet das Ikuyo Mitsuhashi Atelier
1984	Eintritt in das Studio 80
1987	Auszeichnung mit dem Glass Design Grand Prize des NSG Shop & Display Contest
1991 –	Lehrauftrag an der Musashino Art University

PUBLIKATIONEN
Studio 80/1985/G. PAM
Interiors of Uchida, Mitsuhashi & Studio 80/1987/
Rikuyosha Publishing Inc.
Hotel Il PALAZZO – A City Stimulated by
Architecture – /1990/Rikuyosha Publishing Inc.
(Co-Autor)

1944	Naissance à Tokyo
1966	Diplôme de la Tama Art University, Tokyo
1970	Rejoint le Uchida Design Studio
1977	Crée le Ikuyo Mitsuhashi Atelier
1984	Rejoint le Studio 80
1987	Obtient le Glass Design Grand Prize du NSG Shop & Display Contest
1991 –	Conférencière à la Musashino Art University

PUBLICATIONS
Studio 80/1985/G. PAM
Interiors of Uchida, Mitsuhashi & Studio 80/1987/
Rikuyosha Publishing Inc.
Hotel IL PALAZZO – A City Stimulated by
Architecture – /1990/Rikuyosha Publishing Inc.
(coauteur)

Toru Nishioka

1945	Born in Beijing
1967	Graduated from Kuwasawa Design School in Tokyo
1970	Established Nakada-Nishioka Design
1973	Established Nishioka Design Studio
1973 –	Lecturer at Kuwasawa Design School
1981	Established Studio 80
1988	Permanent Collection: ALCEED desk accessories/ The Metropolitan Museum of Art, New York

PUBLICATIONS
Studio 80/1985/G. PAM
Interiors of Uchida, Mitsuhashi & Studio 80/1987/
Rikuyosha Publishing Inc.

1945	Geboren in Peking
1967	Studienabschluß an der Kuwasawa Design School in Tokio
1970	Gründet das Studio Nakada-Nishioka Design
1973	Gründet das Nishioka Design Studio
1973 –	Lehrauftrag an der Kuwasawa Design School
1981	Gründet das Studio 80
1988	Aufnahme der Schreibaccessoires der Serie ALCEED in die Sammlung des New Yorker Metropolitan Museum of Art

PUBLIKATIONEN
Studio 80/1985/G. PAM
Interiors of Uchida, Mitsuhashi & Studio 80/1987/
Rikuyosha Publishing Inc.

1945	Naissance à Pékin
1967	Diplôme de la Kuwasawa Design School, Tokyo
1970	Crée Nakada-Nishioka Design
1973	Crée le Nishioka Design Studio
1973 –	Conférencier à la Kuwasawa Design School
1981	Crée le Studio 80
1988	Ses accessoires de bureaux ALCEED figurent dans la collection permanente du Metropolitan Museum of Art, New York

PUBLICATIONS
Studio 80/1985/G. PAM
Interiors of Uchida, Mitsuhashi & Studio 80/1987/
Rikuyosha Publishing Inc.

Yoshimi Tanaka, Masayuki Kato, Toyota Horiguchi

Hiroyuki Iwasaki, Kenichi Yokobori, Kiyoshi Hasebe

Izumi Suzuki, Minako Morita, Shiro Nakada

Sumihito Oikawa, Yuki Tanaka, Hiroshi Yoneya

Maki Awatsuji, Keisuke Fujiwara, Keiko Taniguchi

Staff
Mitarbeiter
Equipe

Yoshimi Tanaka

Masayuki Kato

Toyota Horiguchi

Hiroyuki Iwasaki

Kenichi Yokobori

Kiyoshi Hasebe

Izumi Suzuki

Minako Morita

Shiro Nakada

Sumihito Oikawa

Yuki Tanaka

Hiroshi Yoneya

Maki Awatsuji

Keisuke Fujiwara

Keiko Taniguchi

Former Staff
Ehemalige Mitarbeiter
Ancienne Equipe

Yasuchika Sonoda	Toshie Nakai
Hiromasa Uchiyama	Kayoko Iida
Takehiko Yanagisawa	Kumiko Saito
Shoichi Tsukahara	Matteo Remonti
Miwa Hirata	Sanae Nakajima
Akiko Sakakida	Shoji Daidoji
Masahiko Mizuno	Takeshi Sasuga
Yutaka Yoshida	Yukako Mizutani
Yuko Machizawa	Katsuhisa Sano
Katsuhiko Togashi	Kazumi Sakuma
Taeko Hori	Midori Ishii
Muneo Ariga	Kazumi Kosaka
Hiroko Noguchi	Keiko Inagaki
Yoshimi Kono	
Takayuki Hoshina	Jan Russell
Tzu-Keng Lin	Ute Vielberth
Nobuko Okajima	Yumi Masuko
Akio Okuda	Mayumi Watanabe
Toshiya Fukuda	Veronika Langer
Erik Schmid	Jon Hallett
Rei Kamiya	Sabina Donetti
Ikuo Nose	Ryusuke Asai
Tomohiro Eguchi	Yong Jin Shin
Takeshi Shimbo	Reiko Yamazaki
Kentaro Kamada	
Naoko Terazaki	
Satoshi Goto	
Shinko Morishita	
Rieko Sugawara	
Mikiko Tomita	
Tamayo Matsuo	
Emiko Ito	
Yuma Mitsuoka	
Kazufumi Oizumi	

Photographic credits
Fotonachweis
Crédits photographiques

P. 3: Nacása & Partners Inc.
P. 14: Shigeru Uchida
P. 17: Shigeru Uchida
P. 18: Shigeo Okamoto
P. 19: Kenzo Yamamoto
P. 21: Tadahiko Hayashi
P. 22: Shigeo Okamoto
P. 24: Shigeru Uchida
P. 29: Pae So
P. 36: Shigeru Uchida
P. 39–42: Nacása & Partners Inc.
P. 44–48: Nacása & Partners Inc.
P. 49: Toyota Horiguchi
P. 50–53: Nacása & Partners Inc.
P. 54–55: Takayuki Ogawa
P. 56: Takayuki Ogawa
P. 57: Nacása & Partners Inc.
P. 60–70: Nacása & Partners Inc.
P. 72–74: Nacása & Partners Inc.
P. 78–81: Nacása & Partners Inc.
P. 82/83: Takayuki Ogawa
P. 85–87: Nacása & Partners Inc.
P. 88–91: Takayuki Ogawa
P. 93–96: Nacása & Partners Inc.
P. 98–106: Nacása & Partners Inc.
P. 108: Nacása & Partners Inc.
P. 109: Courtesy of Morphos
P. 112–117: Mitsumasa Fujitsuka
P. 118–127: Nacása & Partners Inc.
P. 130–135: Nacása & Partners Inc.
P. 136: Hiroyuki Hirai
P. 138: Takeshi Sasuga
P. 139: Mitsumasa Fujitsuka
P. 140–141: Nacása & Partners Inc.
P. 144–148: Mitsumasa Fujitsuka
P. 150 top left, middle and right: Yoshio Shiratori
P. 150 bottom left, middle and right:
    Yoshio Shiratori
P. 151 top left, middle and right: Yoshio Shiratori
P. 151 bottom left: Yoshio Shiratori
P. 151 bottom middle: Mitsumasa Fujitsuka
P. 151 bottom right: Yoshio Shiratori
P. 152 top left, middle and right: Yoshio Shiratori
P. 152 bottom left: Mitsumasa Fujitsuka
P. 152 bottom middle and right:
    Nacása & Partners Inc.
P. 153 top left: Mitsumasa Fujitsuka
P. 153 top middle: Yoshio Shiratori
P. 153 top right: Mitsumasa Fujitsuka
P. 153 bottom left, middle and right:
    Yoshio Shiratori
P. 154 top left: Yoshio Shiratori
P. 154 top middle: Mitsumasa Fujitsuka
P. 154 bottom left: Mitsumasa Fujitsuka
P. 154 bottom middle: Yoshio Shiratori
P. 154 bottom right: Mitsumasa Fujitsuka
P. 155 top left and middle: Yoshio Shiratori
P. 155 top right, bottom left: Mitsumasa Fujitsuka

P. 155 bottom middle: Nacása & Partners Inc.
P. 155 bottom right: Yoshio Shiratori
P. 156 top left: Nacása & Partners Inc.
P. 156 top middle: Mitsumasa Fujitsuka
P. 156 top right, bottom left, middle and right:
    Nacása & Partners Inc.
P. 157 top left: Yoshio Shiratori
P. 157 top middle: Nacása & Partners Inc.
P. 157 top right: Naoya Ikegami
P. 157 bottom left and middle:
    Nacása & Partners Inc.
P. 157 bottom right: Hiroyuki Hirai
P. 158 top left: Yoshio Shiratori
P. 158 top middle and right:
    Nacása & Partners Inc.
P. 158 bottom left, middle and right:
    Nacása & Partners Inc.
P. 159 top left: Nacása & Partners Inc.
P. 159 top middle: Hiroyuki Hirai
P. 159 top right: Nacása & Partners Inc.
P. 159 bottom left, middle and right:
    Nacása & Partners Inc.
P. 160 top left, middle and right:
    Nacása & Partners Inc.
P. 160 bottom left: Nacása & Partners Inc.
P. 160 bottom middle: Peter Paige
P. 160 bottom right: Nacása & Partners Inc.
P. 161 top left, middle and right:
    Nacása & Partners Inc.
P. 161 bottom left, middle and right:
    Nacása & Partners Inc.
P. 162 top left and middle:
    Nacása & Partners Inc.
P. 162 top right: Sharon Risedorph
P. 162 bottom left, middle and right:
    Nacása & Partners Inc.
P. 163 top left, middle and right:
    Nacása & Partners Inc.
P. 163 bottom middle and right:
    Nacása & Partners Inc.
P. 164 top left: Takayuki Ogawa
P. 164 top middle: Nacása & Partners Inc.
P. 164 top right: Courtesy of Morphos
P. 164 bottom left, middle and right:
    Nacása & Partners Inc.
P. 165 top left: Nacása & Partners Inc.
P. 165 top middle and right:
    Mitsumasa Fujitsuka
P. 165 bottom left and middle:
    Nacása & Partners Inc.
P. 165 bottom right: Hiroyuki Hirai
P. 166 top left: Nacása & Partners Inc.
P. 166 top middle and right: Takayuki Ogawa
P. 166 bottom left, middle and right:
    Takayuki Ogawa
P. 167 top left: Takayuki Ogawa
P. 167 top middle and right:
    Nacása & Partners Inc.

P. 167 bottom left, middle and right:
    Nacása & Partners Inc.
P. 168 top left and middle:
    Nacása & Partners Inc.
P. 168 top right: Takayuki Ogawa
P. 168 bottom left: Takayuki Ogawa
P. 168 bottom middle and right:
    Nacása & Partners Inc.
P. 169 top left and middle: Takayuki Ogawa
P. 169 top right: Nacása & Partners Inc.
P. 169 bottom left: Nacása & Partners Inc.
P. 169 bottom middle: Takayuki Ogawa
P. 169 bottom right: Takeshi Sasuga
P. 170 top left, middle and right:
    Nacása & Partners Inc.
P. 170 bottom left, middle and right:
    Nacása & Partners Inc.
P. 171 top left and middle:
    Nacása & Partners Inc.
P. 171 top right: Hiroshi Yoneya
P. 171 bottom left, middle and right:
    Nacása & Partners Inc.
P. 172: Toyota Horiguchi
P. 175: Toyota Horiguchi

We wish to thank the above-mentioned photographers and the following organizations for their kind cooperation.

Acerbis International
Rokuharamitsuji Temple
Sekai Bunka-sha
Shotenkenchiku-sha
Sogetsu Shuppan inc.
The Imperial Household Agency, Kyoto Office